SOCIETY FOR NEW TESTAMENT STUDIES
MONOGRAPH SERIES
General Editor: R.McL. Wilson, F.B.A.
Associate Editor: M.E. Thrall

50

LUKE AND THE LAW

Luke and the Law

S.G. WILSON
Professor of Religion
Carleton University, Ottawa

CAMBRIDGE UNIVERSITY PRESS

CAMBRIDGE
LONDON · NEW YORK · NEW ROCHELLE
MELBOURNE · SYDNEY

Published by the Press Syndicate of the University of Cambridge
The Pitt Building, Trumpington Street, Cambridge CB2 1RP
32 East 57th Street, New York, NY 10022, USA
296 Beaconsfield Parade, Middle Park, Melbourne 3206, Australia

First published 1983

Printed in Great Britain at the University Press, Cambridge

Library of Congress catalogue card number: 83-7263

British Library Cataloguing in Publication Data
Wilson, Stephen G.
Luke and the law. – (Monograph series/Society
for New Testament Studies; 50)
1. Bible. N.T.Luke   2. Jewish law
I. Title   II. Series
296.1'8   BS2595.2
ISBN 0 521 25284 9

WD

CONTENTS

PREFACE

Professors C.K. Barrett, L. Gaston and C.H. Talbert were kind enough to read this work in manuscript form. From them and from the editors of the series, Professor R.McL. Wilson and Dr M.E. Thrall, I received both encouragement and a number of useful suggestions. Professor Wilson and the present associate editor Professor G.N. Stanton were also most helpful in checking the proofs. My thanks to them all and to the efficient and courteous staff at Cambridge University Press.

Unfortunately the commentaries by J.A. Fitzmeyer on Luke (vol. I), and J. Roloff and G. Schneider on Acts were published after the manuscript was complete so that they could not be included in the discussion.

The book is dedicated to my children, without whom I might have written more. They thus bring not only great pleasure to me but great relief to the scholarly world.

S.G. Wilson

ABBREVIATIONS

ANRW	*Aufstieg und Niedergang der römischen Welt*, ed. H. Temporini and W. Haase
ARW	*Archiv für Religionswissenschaft*
BC	*The Beginnings of Christianity*, ed. F.J. Foakes-Jackson, K. Lake, H.J. Cadbury
BJRL	*Bulletin of the John Rylands Library*
Ev. Th.	*Evangelische Theologie*
JBL	*Journal of Biblical Literature*
JSJ	*Journal for the Study of Judaism*
JSNT	*Journal for the Study of the New Testament*
NT	*Novum Testamentum*
NTS	*New Testament Studies*
PW	*Real-Encyclopädie der klassischen Altertumswissenschaft*, ed. H. Pauly, G. Wissowa, W. Kroll
Rev. Qum.	*Revue de Qumran*
SB	*Kommentar zum Neuen Testament aus Talmud und Midrasch*, H.L. Strack and P. Billerbeck
SLA	*Studies in Luke–Acts*, ed. by L.E. Keck and J.L. Martyn
Stud. Theol.	*Studia Theologica*
TDNT	*Theological Dictionary of the New Testament*, ed. G. Kittel and G. Friedrich
Theol. Stud.	*Theological Studies*
TU	*Texte und Untersuchungen zur Geschichte der altchristlichen Literatur*
ZNW	*Zeitschrift für die neutestamentliche Wissenschaft*
ZTK	*Zeitschrift für Theologie und Kirche*

To
Claire, Matthew and Emily

1 LEGAL TERMINOLOGY IN LUKE–ACTS

The use and distribution of three terms are of particular significance for Luke's understanding of the law: 'law' (νόμος), and the associated terms 'custom' (ἔθος) and 'Moses'. The term 'commandment' (ἐντολή) is used in connection with the law only three times (Lk. 1:6; 18:20; 23:56), refers elsewhere to human commands (Lk. 15:29, Ac. 17:15) and need detain us no further.

The term νόμος is not used in Mark, but is found eight times in Matthew and nine in Luke. Five of the occurrences in Luke are found in the birth narratives (Lk. 2:22, 23, 24, 27, 39), two are shared with Matthew (Lk. 16:16, 17; Matt. 5:18; 11:13), and two are in special Lucan material (Lk. 10:26; 24:44). In Acts νόμος is used fifteen times (excluding the variant in 24:6) and of these two are connected with Stephen (6:13; 7:53) and thirteen with Paul (13:15, 39; 15:5; 18:13, 15; 21:20, 24, 28; 22:3, 12; 23:3, 28; 24:14; 25:8; 28:23). The distribution within Acts is itself a significant preliminary indication of the context within which Luke found the law problematic, and is supported by a similar distribution of the related terms 'Moses' and 'custom'.

A survey of the occurrences of νόμος in Luke–Acts suggests that they fall into two main categories. The majority refer to the prescriptions of the law in such phrases as 'the law of the Lord' (Lk. 2:23–4, 39), 'the law of Moses' (Lk. 2:22; Ac. 15:5; 13:39), 'the customs of the law' (Lk. 2:27) or simply 'the law' (Lk. 10:26; 16:17; Ac. 7:53; 13:15; 18:13, 15; 21:20, 24, 28; 22:3, 12; 23:3, 29; 25:8). The remainder speak of the predictive aspect of the law (Lk. 24:44; Ac. 24:14; 28:23; possibly Lk. 16:16), always in connection with 'the prophets', and normally with reference to their presentiment of the fate of Jesus. Both categories will be explored later, but at this stage it is sufficient to note that in linguistic terms Luke's use of νόμος is not unique. It reflects normal Jewish and Christian usage.[1]

Much the same is true of the connection between Moses and the law. A variety of phrases are used: 'the law of Moses' (Lk. 2: 22; 24:44; Ac. 13:39; 15:5 cf. 7:38), 'Moses' (Lk. 20:28, 37; 5:14; Ac. 3:22; 6:11; 15:21;

21:21), 'Moses and the prophets' (Lk. 16:29, 31; 24:27, 44; Ac. 26:22; 28:23 cf. Ac. 7:37), and 'the customs of Moses' (Ac. 6:14; 15:1 cf. Ac. 21:21). Of the above, three references to Moses in the Gospel are shared with Mark (Lk. 5:14; 20:28, 37) and five occur only in Luke (2:22; 16:29, 31; 24:27, 44). Like νόμος, they also fall into two main categories – those which emphasize the prescriptive (Lk. 2:22; 5:14; 16:29, 31; 20:28; Ac. 6:11, 14; 13:39; 15:1, 5; 21:21) and those which display the predictive aspects of Mosaic law (Lk. 24:27, 44; Ac. 3:22; 7:37; 26:22; 28:23 cf. Ac. 7:52).

In view of the frequent connection of Moses with the law, other allusions to Moses in Luke–Acts can be considered, although they are more difficult to categorize. Ac. 15:21, a notoriously obscure statement, at least makes it clear that the peculiarly Lucan allusion to the preaching (κηρύσσω) of Moses in the synagogues does not refer to the predictive, christological interpretation of the law. The significance of the appearance of Moses and Elijah at the Transfiguration (Lk. 9:30, 33) is not wholly clear. Whatever the original intention, it may be that for Luke they symbolize the law (Moses) and the prophets (Elijah) and especially the predictive aspect of these writings. Luke adds the information that 'they spoke of his departure which he was to accomplish at Jerusalem' (9:31) and it is precisely this complex of events which Luke is most concerned to show was a fulfilment of the law and the prophets (Lk. 24:27, 44).[2] Moreover, the wording of Lk. 9:35 (αὐτοῦ ἀκούετε) may be intended as an allusion to the prediction of the Mosaic eschatological prophet (Dt. 18:15 LXX),[3] especially in view of the unambiguous references to this notion in Ac. 3:22; 7:37. In the thumbnail sketch of Moses' career in Ac. 7:20–44 he appears in a variety of roles: as the leader and deliverer of his people (7:22f) who met with opposition and rejection (7:25, 27f, 35, 39f, cf. 7:52–3), as the prophet who announces his own successor (7:37) and as lawgiver (7:38). The last two dovetail with the prophetic/predictive categories, yet neither is the main theme of the speech. They are subsumed under the theme of the divinely appointed leader rejected by his people – as can be seen above all in the concluding remarks (7:52–3).[4]

The association of Moses with the law is, of course, common enough in the Old Testament and in Jewish and Christian writings. Much of Luke's language is not unprecedented, though he does show a penchant for certain expressions. Thus νόμος Μωϋσέως is used five times by Luke (Lk. 2:22; 24:44; Ac. 13:39; 15:5; 28:23) and only three times elsewhere in the New Testament (Jn 7:23; I Cor. 9:9; Heb. 10:28); and the use of 'Moses' to refer to the law in general rather than to a specific command is more frequent in Luke than elsewhere in the New Testament (Lk. 5:14;

16:29, 31; 24:27, 44; Ac. 6:11; 15:1, 21; 21:21; Jn 5:45; 7:22; II Cor. 3:15; Heb. 7:14).

J. Jervell believes that, despite Moses' role as a prophetic figure in Ac. 3:22; 7:37, Luke thinks of him primarily as a lawgiver.[5] However, the overall impression of Ac. 7:20f and the occasions when (in addition to Ac. 3:22; 7:37) the allusion to Moses and the prophets is to their predictive function, suggest otherwise. Certainly Moses as lawgiver is important, but it is not the dominant aspect of Luke's presentation and is but briefly described in Ac. 7:38. Moses as prophet is an equally important theme. It is interesting to note that the most frequent nomenclature for Moses in Philo and Josephus (νομοθέτης)[6] is nowhere used by Luke and that there are no allusions to the expectation of an eschatological reinterpretation of the Torah,[7] even though Luke is the only New Testament writer unambiguously to identify Jesus with the Mosaic eschatological prophet.

In depicting Moses as mediator of the law Luke describes the revelation as 'living oracles' (λόγια ζῶντα Ac. 7:38) and declares that it was 'delivered by angels'. The phrase 'living oracles' appears to be without exact parallel, although a similar connection of ideas appears in Dt. 32:47 where 'doing all the words of the law' is said to be the essential precondition of 'life' or 'a long life' (cf. Lev. 18:5). This may be Luke's point too,[8] the immediate contrast being with Israel's refusal to obey the life-giving words; or he may have understood the λόγια to be the Old Testament prophecies which find their fulfilment in Christ (cf. verse 37). Since Luke may be using a source for Stephen's speech and may have been more concerned with the overall theme than the precise meaning of each verse, exegetical details remain obscure and we certainly cannot assume that by describing the law as 'living oracles' Luke had wholly positive expectation for the function of the law in the Christian era (contrast, e.g., Ac. 13:39; 15:11). Although Jewish literature develops in various ways the information that angels were present on Mt Sinai, they are not assigned the role of mediators,[9] and even if Josephus *Ant.* XV.136 does offer a parallel, which is far from certain, it does not refer to events on Mt Sinai. The only unambiguous references are in Gal. 3:19 and Heb. 2:2f, both of which make a quite different point from Luke: for him it indicates the divine provenance and authority of the law and serves to emphasize the enormity of Israel's disobedience, whereas in Gal. 3:19 and Heb. 2:2f it serves to denigrate the law and subordinates it to the revelation of Christ (cf. II Cor. 3:1f). The negative use of this notion would, of course, have been unsuitable in Stephen's speech, insofar as it would have confirmed the accusations made against him, and Luke at any rate shows no inclination elsewhere to denigrate the law in this fashion.

Unique to Luke in the New Testament are the curious uses of the con-

cept 'custom' in connection with law. The verb ἐθίζω occurs only once
(Lk. 2:27), in the phrase κατὰ τὸ ἐθισμένον τοῦ νόμου with reference to
Jesus' presentation in the Temple. The noun ἔθος is used in the sense of
'habit' (Lk. 22:39 cf. εἴωθα in Lk. 4:16; Ac. 17:2) and with reference to
Roman customs (Ac. 25:16), while the remaining eight occurrences refer
to Jewish customs (Lk. 1:9; 2:42; Ac. 6:14; 15:1; 16:21; 21:21; 26:3;
28:17). In three instances the 'custom' is specified – customs of the priest-
hood (Lk. 1:9), circumcision (Ac. 15:1), passover (Lk. 2:42) – the first of
these recalling rabbinic rather than Old Testament legislation. The others
refer in general to the Jewish way of life, described variously as 'customs'
(Ac. 16:21; 21:21; 26:3), 'the customs of our fathers' (Ac. 28:17) or 'the
customs of Moses' (Ac. 6:14; 15:1 cf. 21:21).

Two observations can be made about this terminology: first, the
phrases 'custom of the law' and 'custom of Moses' seem to be without
parallel in early Christian literature; and second, it is quite clear that Luke
identifies custom and law in Lk. 2:27; Ac. 6:11–14; 15:1, 5; 21:21, and
that this is already implied by the references to specific legal requirements
in Lk. 1:9; 2:42. In Lk. 2:27 ἐθίζω and νόμος are combined in the same
phrase. Ac. 6:14, relating the charge that Stephen proclaimed that 'Jesus
will destroy this Temple and will change the customs which Moses
delivered to us', is clearly synonymous with the variations 'we have heard
him speak words against Moses and God' (6:11) and 'this man never ceases
to speak words against this holy place and the law' (6:13). Similarly, the
'customs of Moses' in Ac. 15:1 seem to be the same as the 'law of Moses'
in 15:5, while in Ac. 21:21 refusing circumcision and disobeying the
customs are equivalent to 'forsaking Moses'.[10]

It would appear that for Luke, on some occasions, the terms ἔθος and
νόμος are interchangeable and that he moves naturally from the one to the
other in describing the same phenomenon. The occurrences are scattered
in a way that does not suggest dependence on a source, so that as a unique
and characteristic usage it is worth exploration to see whether it is significant and to what we may liken it. Heb. 10:25 uses ἔθος to mean 'habit'
(cf. Lk. 22:39; I Macc. 10:89; II Macc. 13:4; Mart. Pol. 9:2), while Jn
19:40 refers to 'the burial customs of the Jews' (cf. II Macc. 11:25; IV
Macc. 18:5 variant). The LXX, apart from the four in the books of
Maccabees mentioned above, contains no other uses of the term.

Rabbinic literature offers equally few parallels.[11] They respected custom (*minhag*) and were aware of its force, and the connection between
Torah, oral law and custom was intimate: 'Even in regard to commandments of the Torah, terms denoting custom are used to indicate their binding nature, which in turn is revealed by custom.'[12] Custom was seen as a

powerful force conditioning men's response to the law (Yeb. 102*a*) and
indicating how far the application of a commandment extended. Variations in local custom were in general respected – for example the peculiar
customs of Jerusalemites (BB 93*b*; Suk. 41*b*; Sanh. 23*a*) which differed
from those of diaspora Jews (Ber. 4*b*) – as long as they did not infringe
specific laws (cf. Pes. 50*b*–57*b*). Custom could fill a halakic void, as when
judges were advised to follow local custom when unsure how a case should
be handled (Ber. 45*a*). It is important to note, however, that although it
could be sacred and binding, custom was never confused with legislation.
Yeb. 13*b*, Nidd. 66*a* distinguish between custom and prohibition, while
Ta'an 26*b* places custom and halakah on quite different levels. This distinction is preserved in the saying 'custom supersedes halakah', the force
of which is open to some dispute. It refers to two specific cases (p.B. Metz.
11*b*, p. Yeb. 12*c*), one dealing with a dispute between sages and the other
with local custom and, according to Falk, 'no ground is furnished for the
view that custom really superseded halakah in torts or in prohibition and
permission'.[13] The issue is discussed in Soph. 14:18: 'As to the saying of
the Rabbis that "custom supersedes halakah", it applies to a custom of
the Elders; but custom which has no support from the Torah is like a
mere injudicious decision.' This apparently reflects a controversy over the
role of custom – perhaps an earlier, popular rejection of halakah in favour
of custom, which the Amoraim later explain as itself based on halakah.
The sense seems to be that halakah can be superseded only by proof from
the Torah or a decision of the Elders. Both the Amoraic view and the
view they are probably opposing, however, work with a clear distinction
between law/halakah and custom. To this extent, and to the extent
that this late evidence is of relevance to the end of the first century,
rabbinic literature provides no useful parallel to Luke's peculiar linguistic
usage.

Philo uses ἔθος of foreign customs (*Somn.* II.56; *Spec. Leg.* III.13) and
of the variety of customs among different peoples (*Ebr.* 193; *Jos.* 29). In
many passages ἔθος and νόμος are mentioned together and clearly dis-
tinguished (*Leg. All.* III.30, 43; *Quod Deus* 17; *Somn.* II.78) and in one
instance custom is compared unfavourably with law (*Mut. Nom.* 104). His
attitude towards custom seems ambivalent, since he oscillates between
praise and disparagement. Certain customs, especially those of non-Jews,
he views as degrading and superstitious (*Rer. Div.* 279; *Virt.* 218–19;
Congr. Ed. 85; *Spec. Leg.* III.29), but he also makes disparaging remarks
about custom in general. When contrasting the influence of reason and
custom on human behaviour, he declares that 'obedience to custom is the
special property of women; indeed custom is the rule of the weaker and

more effeminate soul' (*Ebr.* 55). On the other hand, his evaluation of
Jewish customs is often favourable, perhaps most clearly in *Spec. Leg.*
IV.149 where custom is praised as an adjunct to law and parents are
encouraged to instill respect for it in their offspring. The danger, it appears,
was that customs would be despised because they did not have the force of
written law. At this point he defines custom: 'For customs are unwritten
laws, the decisions approved by the men of old (ἔθη γὰρ ἄγραφοι νόμοι,
δόγματα παλαιῶν ἀνδρῶν), not inscribed on monuments nor on leaves of
paper which the moth destroys, but on the souls of those who are partners
in the same citizenship.' A similar definition is found in *Leg.* 115–16:
Jews are taught by their 'sacred laws and also the unwritten customs (τῶν
ἀγράφων ἐθῶν)'. In neither context does Philo give specific examples of
these customs, but it is clear that while custom can be defined as a kind of
law, the essential distinction between ἔθος and νόμος remains.

Yet even this distinction is occasionally overlooked when Philo defines
practices which are prescribed in the law as 'customs' – circumcision
(*Spec. Leg.* I.3), passover (*Spec. Leg.* II.148), and sacrifices (*Vit. Mos.*
I.87). Indeed, *Leg. ad Gaium* 210 comes close to identifying the two
terms: 'All men guard their customs (ἔθη), but especially the Jews. Hold-
ing that the laws (νόμοι) are oracles vouchsafed from God . . . ' General
references to Jewish customs, which mark them off from other people
(*Vit. Mos.* I.278) yet gain them respect (*In Flacc.* 47), probably include
things like circumcision, sabbath observance and dietary rules which were
the immediately visible signs of Jewish allegiance. It would thus appear
that on occasions the distinction between custom and law collapses,
especially in apologetic contexts where Philo defends a particular Jewish
practice (*Spec. Leg.* I.3), or Jewish customs in general, to the non-Jewish
world. This tendency is understandably more prominent in *Legatio ad
Gaium* than in any other of Philo's writings. While within Judaism it was
clear that these practices had the force of law, a plea for tolerance was
more likely to be effective if they were presented as ancient, well-
established customs such as are exhibited by all national groups.

The same ploy is used more frequently and more consistently by
Josephus. He uses the term ἔθος 166 times and an indication of his interest
in custom is the promised treatise on *Customs and Causes* which unfortunately he never compiled (*Bell.* V.237; *Ant.* IV.198). Occasionally he
uses ἔθος of non-Jewish customs – Egyptian (*Ant.* I.166; *Ap.* II.10, 139,
142), Samaritan (*Ant.* IX.290; XIII.259–61) and Roman (*Bell.* III.115;
IV.13; V.402, etc.) – but the majority of references refer to Jewish
customs. Included are a wide variety of customs covered by the law:
annual festivals (*Bell.* I.26; II.410; VI.299, 300; *Ant.* II.313), sacrifices

(*Bell.* I.153; *Ant.* XII.324), the sabbath (*Bell.* II.392; *Ant.* XIV.245–6; *Ap.* II.282), circumcision (*Ant.* I.214), etc., as well as specifically Essene (*Bell.* II.143, 160–1) and Nazirite practices (*Bell.* II.313). More generally, ἔθος describes the Jewish way of life as a whole, which distinguishes the Jews from other peoples (*Bell.* VII.50; *Ant.* IV.137, VIII.192, XX.58, 71, 139), and which was proscribed by Antiochus (*Ant.* XII.255, 271) and defended by various Roman rulers (*Ant.* XVI.171–6; XIV.213–16, 245–6; XIX.283–90, 306–11).

It frequently seems that Josephus uses ἔθος and νόμος as synonyms. He contrasts the observance of 'the sabbath custom' with transgression of 'ancestral laws' (*Bell.* II.392–3). Mattathias urges his sons 'to preserve our customs . . . die for our laws . . . and you shall live securely and enjoy our customs' (*Ant.* XII.281). Hyrcanus' appointment as High Priest is described as being 'in accord with our national customs' or 'in accord with their own laws' (*Ant.* XIV.194 and 195). In a Roman declaration of Jewish rights 'doing all those things which are in accord with their native customs' is apparently the equivalent of 'doing all those things which are in accord with their own laws' (*Ant.* XIV.263–4).

It might appear that for Josephus ἔθος and νόμος are interchangeable terms, useful for stylistic variation. Yet there are times, especially where the 'customs and laws' of the Jews are mentioned in a single phrase, when we would not immediately suppose them to be equivalent (*Bell.* II.195; V.237; *Ant.* XI.217; XVI.43). Josephus' use of ἔθος may, of course, be imprecise, or he may have intended to give a more exact definition in his treatise on *Customs and Causes*. There are at any rate a few passages which suggest how that definition might have been made. In *Ap.* II.155f Josephus considers the customs and laws of the Jews in the light of the endless variety of customs which prevail in the world at large (164f). The Greeks, like many ancient peoples, depended on unwritten customs (ἔθη ἄγραφα) which, precisely for that reason, were both vague and changeable. The Jews, by contrast, had the law of Moses, one of whose advantages was that it was written and unchangeable. Although Josephus does not specifically make the point, since he is contrasting Jewish and foreign practices, he might be implying that within Judaism 'custom' and 'law' are two different ways of looking at the same phenomena. The Jews have distinctive customs as do all national groups, but theirs have the additional advantage of being defined and upheld by a written law. For the sake of comparison with other peoples, Jewish practices can be defined as customs, but from another point of view they are seen to be legally binding. A similar sense is conveyed by *Ant.* IV.198f, which gives a summary of the 'laws' of Moses 'as they touch upon our political institution'. The remaining material Josephus reserves for his unwritten treatise on 'custom', the content of which is described as the 'further laws of Moses' (cf. *Bell.* V.237). Here, it would seem, the content of the planned treatise is described as both custom and law, and there is no suggestion that these refer to two different elements within it. It would seem, therefore, that Josephus can describe the same practices as both Jewish custom and Jewish law. Observance of the sabbath and food laws, for example, are Jewish customs well-known to, and often emulated by, non-Jews (*Ap.* II.282f); but Jews observed them not only out of force of habit or because they were deemed sensible and useful, but also because they were written in the Torah. In this connection we might note that Josephus uses the distinction between written laws and unwritten customs not, like Philo, to distinguish different practices within Judaism, but to contrast Jewish practices with those of other peoples.

The association of ἔθος and νόμος in Josephus has rarely evoked comment. It has been suggested that his view that customs are part of the law 'shows his orientation to Pharisaism'.[14] Certainly Josephus, by his own account, was trained as a Pharisee, and we have seen that in his summaries of the law he often refers to practices not covered by Torah legislation, some of which reappear in later rabbinic discussions (*Ant.* IV; *Ap.* II). However, insofar as we can use rabbinic evidence to characterize Pharisaism, it is significant that rabbinic literature clearly distinguishes custom and law in a way that Josephus does not; and, moreover, many of the Jewish practices which Josephus designates as custom are also covered by Torah legislation. Thus Josephus' Pharisaic background does not appear to explain his understanding of custom.

It seems that we must look to a quite different background for an explanation, namely Josephus' apology on behalf of Judaism in the Roman world. The Jews were frequently ridiculed, occasionally persecuted and constantly engaged in civic disputes. They were, of course, by no means always the innocent victims. The various skirmishes in the first century, culminating in the war of 66–70 C.E., did not endear them to the Roman authorities. The resulting ill-will and suspicion was, however, temporary and may not have affected many diaspora communities at all. Yet there was a widespread and more fundamental anti-Jewish sentiment with which any literate apologist had to contend. To the non-Jew the Jews appeared to be a strange and stubborn people, fanatically committed to the preservation of their eccentric beliefs and customs.[15] Religious observances such as the sabbath, circumcision and food laws were immediately recognizable and naturally attracted most attention. Sabbath observance and circumcision led to charges of idleness and brutality. Their monotheistic and aniconic tradition led them to be suspected of atheism and impiety and caused particular difficulty with the Emperor cult. When granted special dispensation, as they were in the case of Emperor worship, this merely fuelled resentment and suspicion. In many cities, such as Rome and Alexandria, they chose to live in a Jewish quarter, thus encouraging the view that their disapproval of non-Jews was matched only by their excessive loyalty to each other. Such a view of Judaism was in all probability not universal and the evidence may often represent the views of a literate minority, but it is sufficient to show that to some the Jews appeared as people with strange customs, an objectionable lifestyle, and incomprehensible beliefs – and this they were not slow to point out.

It is in this context that we must place the use of ἔθος in Josephus and, to a lesser extent, Philo. Josephus pleads for a measure of understanding and tolerance of Jewish customs and beliefs in the Roman world. An important part of his strategy was to present Jewish 'customs' as equivalent to the peculiar customs proper to all peoples. In *Ant.* XVI.35f, Nicolas of Damascus defends Jewish rights before Agrippa by pointing out that Jews are no different from other men in that they would prefer to go to war and suffer all manner of things than to violate their ancestral customs. He refers to the praiseworthy Roman practice of allowing their subjects religious freedom – a point which Josephus frequently underlines by his quotation of Imperial decrees setting out the religious rights of the Jews (*Ant.* XIV.213–16, 245–6; XVI.171–6; XIX.283–90, 306–11). Different peoples, Josephus claims, should be allowed to follow different customs as long as they encourage the pursuit of goodness (*Ant.* XVI.176f). Jewish customs not only encourage piety and righteousness and are thus worthy of veneration (*Ant.* XVI.43–7) – not to mention the fact that they are widely respected and even emulated by non-Jews (*Ant.* III.217; *Ap.* II.282). Sensitive to the delicate position of Judaism in the pagan world, Josephus thus projects an ideal of toleration and respect for men's customs. This places an obligation not only upon the Gentiles but also upon the Jews, who are reminded that they should not blaspheme the gods of other nations nor abuse the gifts offered to them (*Ant.* IV.207; *Ap.* II.237 cf. Philo *Spec. Leg.* I.52–3; *Vit. Mos.* II.203–6).[16]

For Josephus, therefore, ἔθος was not only a descriptive but also an apologetic term. He used it to locate the religious observances of Judaism within the broader context of national customs and at the same time to appeal for tolerance. The interchangeable use of ἔθος and νόμος clearly does not distinguish between written and unwritten laws, but neither was it intended to blur that distinction. It was rather the linguistic expression of Josephus' attempt to find an acceptable niche for Judaism in the

Roman world by presenting it in terms which would be comprehensible to an outsider and which would dispel common misconceptions. Josephus was well aware that within Judaism ancestral customs were reinforced by written law, but to an outsider the practices based on Jewish law were best explained as customs different in kind, but not in principle, from those of other peoples. In a sense the uses of ἔθος and νόμος also express the ambivalence of Josephus' own position as a man with a foot in two worlds. The transition from Pharisee and Jewish military commander to Imperial Court pensioner and historian meant that, while still capable of a spirited defence of Judaism (*Apion*), he nevertheless was somewhat removed from the Jews of his day and was able, too, to understand how Judaism was viewed from the outside.

Is it possible that Josephus and Philo shed some light on Luke's use of ἔθος and νόμος? It should be noted first that there is no exact parallel to the Lucan phrases 'customs of the law' or 'customs of Moses' in the literature surveyed, and a study of related terms such as ἦθος, ἔθειν and εἴωθα in Jewish and Christian literature adds nothing to the information gained from the use of ἔθος. There is no reason to suppose that Luke was influenced by the rabbinic view of custom which presupposes a clear distinction between custom and law, or by Philo's definition of custom as 'unwritten laws' which is part of his general denigration of custom.

It is in the writings of Josephus, and to a more limited degree Philo, where ἔθος and νόμος are often used interchangeably, that we come closest to Luke's usage. There is no explicit apologetic on behalf of Jewish customs/laws in Luke of the sort that is especially evident in Josephus – no attempt to describe and justify particular practices, no appeal based on the analogy with other national customs and, incidentally, no attempt to prove the superiority of the Jewish way of life. It may be, however, that Luke shares the cosmopolitan tone and cultural magnanimity common to Josephus and Philo. Like Josephus, Luke can use ἔθος to describe practices which are covered by legislation in the Torah as well as some which are not. In neither case does it imply any disrespect for the law but is rather an attempt to set the customs/laws of the Jews in a broader cultural context. Does Luke's usage contain an implicit (as Josephus' contains an explicit) invitation to the reader to view Jewish practices in the same way as those of other peoples and accord them the same respect?

Of course, describing the ways of the Jews as customs is not confined to Jewish writers. Dio refers to those who were converted to Jewish customs (*Hist.* LVII.14.2, 18.52) and to the observance of Jewish customs after 70 C.E. (*Hist.* LXV.9.2), and Diodorus contains a reference to the 'customs and laws' of the Jews (XL.3.1–8) as well as a few more hostile references to their practices (e.g. I.55.5). It is worth noting too that the only parallel use of ἔθος in the LXX (II Macc. 11:25; IV Macc. 18:5 is a variant reading) is ostensibly part of a letter by a non-Jew, Antiochus V, in which he rescinds his father's decision forcibly to hellenize the Jews. To this we might add the use of the same term in the Imperial edicts quoted by Josephus which defend Jewish rights (e.g. *Ant.* XIV.213–16, 245–6; XVI.171–6), even though their authenticity is a matter of dispute. This evidence is sufficient to show that non-Jews quite naturally described Jewish practices as 'customs' and makes sense of Josephus' attempt to use this for apologetic reasons.

　　J. Jervell characterizes Luke's legal terminology as 'conservative and Jewish', and by the latter he means non-biblical.[17] That it is 'Jewish' is true in most respects but that it is conservative seems not to be the case, at least with the characteristically Lucan use of ἔθος. Whichever analogy is thought to be more appropriate for this usage, hellenistic–Jewish or non-Jewish, a similar impression is conveyed. To describe the law as ἔθος is to view it as a cultural as much as a religious phenomenon and indicates an ability to view it either from something of a distance or within a broad perspective. We might go further and suggest that Luke's language implies an attitude towards Jewish law which is both tolerant, in that it upholds the right of the Jews to follow the practices most natural to them, and yet also restrictive, in that it would view as unnatural the imposition of this law where it does not belong, i.e. on Gentiles. Perhaps we have here at least one important insight into Luke's view of the law, and to this we can return after surveying the other pertinent material in Luke–Acts.

My conclusions in Chapter 1 should be compared with those in A. George, 'Israël', in *Etudes sur l'oeuvre Luc* (Paris, 1978), pp. 88–125, which I discovered after the book was in press. He suggests in passing (pp. 119, 122–4) that Luke's use of ἔθος places Jewish law on a par with the customs of other nations, but thinks this reflects Luke's negative judgement on Jews who do not accept the Gospel: they are 'Jews' rather than 'Israelites', with 'customs' rather than 'law'. This is an 'indice de la caducité de la loi juive dans le pensée de Luc' (p. 119). This does not seem, however, to fit the use of ἔθος by either Luke or his contemporaries.

2 LAW IN LUKE'S GOSPEL

The theme of law in Luke's Gospel has not been much discussed. Insofar as the relevant material has been considered it has usually been in the context of an examination of Jesus' view of the law. A notable exception is the essay by J. Jervell and a sketch of this and other views can be found in the conclusion to this chapter. It is a truism, but one that needs constantly to be kept in mind, that it is a quite different matter to enquire after the Lucan understanding of Jesus' view of the law than to trace the same theme in the teaching of the historical Jesus. The situation of Luke and his readers and changes in Jewish practice and belief can significantly alter the picture. Some have thought the theme of law to be of little significance in the third Gospel, but even if there is an element of truth in this judgement it is important and necessary to consider the evidence if we are to gain a complete picture of Luke–Acts.

As a matter of convenience, the pertinent material will be discussed systematically rather than consecutively as it appears in Luke's narrative. This can result in distortion both of the intention of the author, insofar as this is recoverable, and of the impression the narrative would have had on its first readers. Not only is the selection of particular categories an expression of the pre-understanding of the interpreter, but a thematic approach may also give a false impression of coherence to material which is recorded in a haphazard way. We shall have good reason to return to these matters when concluding this chapter.

In discussing the evidence in the Gospel no attempt will be made to explore traditio-historical or source questions in any detail. The primary concern is with the final form of Luke's narrative and the impression it conveys, so that the prior history of the traditions he utilizes will be considered only insofar as it contributes to this purpose. This is perhaps just as well, since there is little consensus and even less certainty about the criteria for and the results of historical analysis. Likewise, no particular theory of synoptic relationships will be assumed. Doubts about the ability of the two-document hypothesis to explain the synoptic problem have been raised by an increasingly vocal minority who, though unable to provide a persuasive counter-proposal, have exposed the weaknesses of many of the arguments used for the priority of Mark. Quite apart from this, however, the assumption of a particular hypothesis about the relationship of the synoptic gospels is not necessary for a consideration of Luke's narrative. A comparison of both individual pericopes and their overall effect in the three gospels can still be made without assuming the priority of one of them, although on occasions the two-document hypothesis may have to be assumed for the sake of argument since these are the terms in which the debate is usually cast. It is safer and simpler not to build on a disputed theory, especially when the end result is much the same. An additional advantage is that this procedure encourages us to avoid a common weakness of redaction criticism, that is, when attention is drawn almost exclusively to material which has demonstrably been altered while the simple repetition of a source is dismissed as part of mere tradition. But whether Luke repeats, alters or conflates his sources, or creates the material himself, he is in each case exercising authorial control and we are obliged to take the end result as the expression of his purpose. Moreover, since we are probably safe in assuming that those for whom Luke wrote did not enjoy his access to alternative accounts, by responding first and foremost to the finished work we put ourselves as best we can into a position comparable to that of his first readers.

A. Doing the law

Perhaps the most obvious place to begin is with the statement in Lk. 16:17:

> But it is easier for heaven and earth to pass away than for one dot of the law to become void.

Considered in isolation it would appear to be a categorical affirmation of the eternal validity of the whole law down to the smallest detail. There is no qualifying phrase such as the ἕως ἂν πάντα γένηται in the Matthean parallel (Matt. 5:18) which, understood temporally or christologically, places some sort of limit on the validity of the law.[1] Luke's statement is absolute and unqualified.[2] At a later stage we shall have to return to this verse and its context but for now it is sufficient to note that it can be, and usually is, understood as a confirmation of the absolute validity of the law in which the phrase 'It is easier for heaven and earth to pass away . . . ' is an idiomatic way of saying 'never'. As such it is unique in Luke's Gospel since, while other material in the Gospel may imply the same view or something close to it, it is the only direct and categorical statement of principle.

Lk. 10:25—8 provides perhaps the best illustration of the assertion in Lk. 16:17. Luke's version diverges significantly from the parallel traditions (Mk. 12:28—34; Matt. 22:34—40), most importantly in the initial question of Jesus' antagonist (γραμματεύς in Mark, νομικός in Matthew and Luke) and in the concluding words of Jesus:

Mk 12:28: Which is the foremost of all the commandments?
Matt. 22:36: Which is the greatest commandment in the law?
Lk. 10:25: What shall I do to inherit eternal life?

Mk 12:34: You are not far from the kingdom of God.
Matt. 22:40: On these two commandments hang all the law and the prophets.
Lk. 10:28: You have answered correctly. Do this and you shall live.

In addition, the summary of the law in terms of the double love command is given in Mark by Jesus and repeated by the lawyer, in Matthew by Jesus alone and in Luke by the lawyer alone. The differences have led some to suppose that Luke follows a different version of the same incident[3] and others to argue that he describes a different incident altogether.[4] Or again, in view of the agreements between Matthew and Luke, some think they had access to a non-Markan tradition[5] which Luke follows closely and Matthew conflates with Mark.[6] While some think that Luke's version is the oldest,[7] others suppose that the scenario of Lk. 10:25 is influenced by Lk. 18:18f and parallels.[8] Since most of these issues cannot be resolved, we shall concentrate upon Luke's narrative as it stands and as it compares with what appear to be parallel traditions in the other gospels.

The striking divergence in the initial question shows that for Luke the issue at stake is not the relative merits of various commandments but how men gain eternal life. The primarily theoretical question in Matthew (though doubtless with practical implications) is replaced by an unambiguously pragmatic question in Luke. His interest in obedience to, rather than discussion about, the law is thus immediately apparent and is reinforced in two further ways. First, Luke shapes the conclusion in line with the wording of the initial question: 'Do this and you shall live.' Similarly, Matthew's conclusion — 'on these two commands hang all the law and the prophets' — confirms his theoretical phrasing of the question where the immediate issue is one of interpretation and assessment of, rather than the necessity of obedience to, the law. In Mark the scribe's repetition of Jesus' summary of the law is contrasted with 'burnt offerings and sacrifice', to the disadvantage of the latter, and his insight is praised with the cautious but

encouraging words, 'You are not far from the kingdom of God.' The difference between Mark and Luke is twofold: it is the man's understanding
rather than his obedience which brings him close to the kingdom; and
whereas in Luke 'doing the law' brings life, i.e. entry into the kingdom, in
Mark understanding the law brings a man close to, but not yet within, the
kingdom. Perhaps doing the law is the extra which guarantees eternal life,
but this Mark does not say.

Luke reinforces his understanding of the pericope, secondly, by his
unique juxtaposition of the discussion with the lawyer and the parable of
the good Samaritan. The summary of the law and Jesus' ensuing exhortation are immediately followed by the question: 'And who is my neighbour?' In the Old Testament 'neighbour' refers to fellow Israelites – a view
which probably prevailed at the time of Jesus and possibly in Luke's day
too.[9] Luke, however, presents it as an attempt to evade the issue by shifting the discussion from a practical to a theoretical plane. The lawyer
attempts to 'justify himself' (verse 29), which refers less to his failure to
keep the law than to his attempt to justify his initial question to which he
apparently knew the answer all along (he 'tempts' Jesus, verse 25). The
parable presents a vivid picture of compassion in which love of neighbour
is described as σπλαγχνίζεσθαι (verse 33) and ποιεῖν ἔλεος (verse 37). At
the same time there is a subtle shift in which 'neighbour' becomes the subject (verse 36) rather than the object (verse 29) of acts of love. The emphasis on the quality of neighbourliness rather than on the quantity of those
who belong to the category 'neighbour' implicitly corrects the presupposition behind the lawyer's question in verse 29, and the discussion is
brought firmly back to the practical plane by the dominical command in
verse 37: 'Go and do likewise.' The Lucan refrain (cf. ποιεῖν in verses 25,
28, 36, 37) could not be clearer.[10] Doing the law rather than discussing
and refining it is the crucial issue.

It would seem that for Luke the law can be adequately summarized in
the two great commands and that obedience to them is sufficient qualification for entry into the kingdom. His emphasis on doing the law rather
than discussing and defining it is such that we might say that the issue
which pervades the Matthean and Markan accounts is specifically rejected
as a false trail in the Lucan version.

It is not clear what we should infer from the appearance of a Samaritan
whose actions are deliberately contrasted with those of the priests and
Levites. In view of the intense mutual suspicion of Jews and Samaritans
and the fact that Samaritans would normally be considered by Jews to be
neither neighbours nor capable of works of love, the choice of a Samaritan
can scarcely be without significance. It is probably a shock tactic, not

uncommon in the parables, designed to jolt the listener from familiar patterns of thought. Perhaps Luke is also implying that belonging to the people of God is no longer the exclusive right of the Jews – it depends no longer on accidents of birth but on obedience to the will of God, and Samaritans and Gentiles can achieve that too (cf. Ac. 10:2, 35). But this, or a proleptic glimpse of the Samaritan and Gentile missions, seems to be at most a peripheral concern in this passage.

Berger suggests that Luke presents salvation as dependent not on obedience to the law but on response to the teaching of Jesus, some of which can be found in the Old Testament when it is read properly, and that he understands love of neighbour primarily in terms of almsgiving.[11] In both cases, however, Berger appears to transfer notions from the admittedly similar passage in Lk. 18:18f. It is particularly significant that in Lk. 10:25f the lawyer summarizes the law, while Jesus merely urges obedience to it and resists his evasive tactics. Moreover, while Luke undoubtedly shows a concern for practical expression of the love command and is frequently exercised about the correct use of wealth, it is not clear that these two should be identified in this passage.

Sellin offers an unusual interpretation of Lk. 10:25–37, which he believes to be the key to Luke's understanding of the law.[12] He rejects interpretations similar to the one above on three grounds.[13] First, they do not explain the choice of a Samaritan as an example of neighbourliness. Second, there is nothing in the preceding story (verses 30–5) to prepare us for the sudden change of perspective in verse 36. Third, such interpretations require that the lawyer identify himself with the Samaritan, whereas the formal protagonist in verses 30–5, as well as verse 36, is the wounded man – thus contradicting a formal rule of dramatic storytelling according to which the listener is to identify with one figure who is from beginning to end the centre of the story. Sellin's own interpretation rests on two main suppositions: that the appearance of a Samaritan is of particular significance; and that 10:36 neither changes the perspective of, nor implicitly corrects, the question in 10:29. As to the latter, he argues, throughout 10:30–7*a* the figure with whom the lawyer is to identify is the wounded man, and the conclusion he is to draw is that even the Samaritan is to be seen as his neighbour. As to the former, the Samaritan is on the one hand contrasted with the priests and Levites who represent Israel – the old, cultically oriented Israel which from Luke's vantage point had disappeared after 70 C.E. – and on the other hand extolled as one who knows and does the law, in line with a rabbinic tradition about the Samaritans current at the end of the first century. A Samaritan rather than a Gentile is used because, although he is in Luke's view a non-Jew (cf. ἀλλογενής Lk.

17:18), he knows the law and thus forms a bridge between Jews and Gentiles, as does the Samaritan mission in Ac. 1:8; 8:1f. In this way Luke can show that the demands of the law are universally applicable – a theme which Sellin connects with Luke's conviction that the Church is the true Israel and with the natural theology of hellenistic Judaism.

Although intriguing, Sellin's argument is in the last resort not convincing. His arguments against the more traditional interpretations of the parable are not persuasive. The formal objections to the purported change of perspective from 10:29 to 10:36 are not conclusive, since one of the consistent features of parable as a literary form is an element of surprise in which the conventional expectations of the audience are unexpectedly reversed and old questions given a new twist – an observation that is pertinent even if Sellin is right in supposing that Lk. 10:29–37 is a Lucan creation. That the Samaritan represents non-Jews who know the law rests, as Sellin recognizes, on the generous view of Samaritans of Rabbi Akiba which was by no means shared by his contemporaries and successors such as Rabbi Eliezer b. Hyrcanus and Rabbi Ishmael,[14] and at any rate depends on the assumption that the ascription of these views is historically reliable. It is true that Luke was favourably disposed towards the Samaritans as was Akiba according to rabbinic tradition, but there is not the slightest indication in Luke that this was because they knew the law. Luke's readers might as readily have assumed that the Samaritan obeyed God's will despite his ignorance, rather than because of his knowledge, of the law. The appearance of the Samaritan challenges Jewish prerogatives not because he knows and does the law, which does not come into play here any more than in Lk. 17:11f, but because as one who is technically a non-Jew, or some form of hybrid, he responds to the divine will more readily than those who claim direct and unique knowledge of it. Finally, if Sellin is right, we must allow for a sudden change of perspective in 10:37*b*, for there is no doubt that the command to 'Go and do likewise' identifies the lawyer with the Samaritan and not with the wounded traveller. Sellin argues that 10:37*b* stands formally outside the parable and serves as a warning to the lawyer that he is in danger of losing his natural heritage. It seems, on the contrary, that verse 37*b* is an indication precisely of Luke's understanding of the parable and concurs with the emphasis on doing the law which characterizes Luke's version of the preceding discussion (verses 25–8).

The double reference to 'Moses and the prophets' in the parable of the rich man and Lazarus (Lk. 16:29, 31) fits smoothly into the views expressed in Lk. 10:25f. The rich man, anxious that his brothers should be warned to avoid his fate, begs Abraham to send Lazarus to them. Abraham replies, 'They have Moses and the prophets, let them hear them', and 'If they do not hear Moses and the prophets neither will they be convinced if someone should rise from the dead.' The clear implication of both verses is that the law and the prophets were an adequate guide for those who wished to enter the kingdom. If the rich man had heard and obeyed, especially though not exclusively with respect to the use of his wealth, he would not have found himself in such dire circumstances. As in 10:25f the emphasis is on 'hearing' (ἀκούειν), that is obeying and doing, the law. Its demands are straightforward. Failure to do them is the result not of any obscurity in or inadequacy of the law but of a stubbornness which even a person raised from the dead could not dispel. It is difficult to think that Luke did not see in verse 31 an allusion to the post-resurrection mission of the Church and the Jews' refusal of its message; but despite men's failure to respond to the law, the positive evaluation stands. There is no reason to suppose that verses 27–31 were a 'serious embarrassment to Luke',[15] for what they imply is elsewhere clearly stated (e.g. 10:25f).

Lk. 11:37–52 contains a critique of Pharisaic and scribal religion, the bulk of which is also found in Matt. 23. Luke's version is briefer, differentiates between woes against Pharisees (verses 37–44) and scribes (verses 45–52), and lacks the recurring charge of hypocrisy which is one of the controlling themes of Matt. 23. Luke's introduction of the material within the setting of a meal seems artificial (cf. Lk. 5:39; 7:36; 10:38) and Jesus is presented as a somewhat ungracious guest (verses 39f)! We shall return to the main theme of this section, but meanwhile a few of the details are worth noting. In verse 42 Jesus contrasts the Pharisees' care over tithing 'mint, rue and allspice' with their neglect of 'justice and the love of God' (παρέρχεσθε τὴν κρίσιν καὶ τὴν ἀγάπην τοῦ θεοῦ). There follows the significant observation: 'These things you ought to have done (ποιῆσαι) and not neglected the others.' The Matthean equivalent (23:23) is somewhat different: mint, dill and cummin are the spices tithed and the contrast is with 'justice, mercy and faith' (κρίσις, ἔλεος, πίστις) defined as 'the weightier matters of the law' (τὰ βαρύτερα τοῦ νομοῦ). Luke contains no explicit reference to the 'weightier matters of the law', which implies that there are less significant matters, although the same contrast is probably intended. The three virtues in Matthew, which refer primarily to human relationships, are replaced with an abbreviated version of the two great commands enunciated in Lk. 10:25f – love of God and love of neighbour.[16]

Certainly these verses are consistent with the generally critical tone of the chapter, but Pharisaic scrupulosity is surprisingly not condemned but condoned. The neglect of essentials alone is denounced. Although tithing was recommended in the law (Lev. 27:30; Num. 18:21, etc.) the application to spices was a Pharisaic innovation. Indeed, mint is not mentioned in later rabbinic regulations (Maas. 4:5; Dem. 2:1) and rue is specifically exempted (Shab. 9:1). Luke apparently saw nothing objectionable in a Pharisaic lifestyle *per se*, including the commitment to an expanded legal system; he objects only to the neglect of central commands, whose centrality they themselves recognized (Lk. 10:25f). This apparent affirmation of Pharisaic tradition has inevitably roused suspicion: some classify it as an extreme Jewish-Christian insertion,[17] others treat it as ironical,[18] and it is occasionally omitted as in the Western text and Marcion.[19] However, the last two suggestions are scarcely convincing, and the first goes beyond the scope of our discussion. Clearly, it must be assessed within its immediate and highly polemical context.[20] It is contradicted elsewhere in Matthew (15:1–11; 23:24) but not so clearly in Luke, although the preceding saying (11:41) might be taken in this way. Nowhere else in Luke do we find a similar affirmation of scribal tradition, since it is usually the two great commands that are in mind when the law is affirmed. Nevertheless, however we explain its origin, it is significant that Luke retains it and that it conforms to his emphasis on doing the law (ποιῆσαι verse 42*b*). Nor does it stand completely alone, for in 11:52 the scribes are accused of 'taking away the key of knowledge; you did not enter yourselves and you hindered those who were entering' (cf. Matt. 23:13). The tone is distinctly hostile, but the implication is that the key of knowledge was accessible to the scribes had they not squandered their chance to possess it. They could have entered the kingdom and led others there too – but they have done neither. Whether in Luke's mind they had obscured the truth by their teaching or behaviour is not clear, though the context suggests the latter. Admittedly, in view of the context we should not overrate what is no more than an implicit possibility. Neither this verse nor verse 42 should be assigned disproportionate significance, since both are somewhat overwhelmed by their surroundings, yet we cannot ignore them altogether.

Before turning to Lucan examples of pious obedience to the law, we should consider the peculiar saying in Lk. 5:39. Following the parables of the patched garment and wineskins (Lk. 5:33–8; Mk 2:18–22; Matt. 9:14–17) come the words: 'No-one who has drunk old wine wants new; for he says, "The old is better".'[21] The preceding parables, themselves obscure, help little in the elucidation of this verse. The gist seems to be that old and new are equally important and worthy of preservation, but both will be spoilt if they are combined. This seems clear from all versions of the second parable, and Luke's wording of the first makes it that much clearer by introducing the notion of taking a patch from a new garment.

H. Schürmann thinks Luke is thus expressing hostility towards both Judaism and the Judaizing movement within Christianity, likening them to an old, torn garment which is no longer of use.[22] But the problem is precisely that we cannot confidently identify the old and the new. Luke probably did understand them broadly, as contrasting Judaism and Christianity in general rather than law and Gospel or Jewish and Gentile Christianity,[23] but there is no note of hostility towards the old. Therefore 5:39 probably alludes to the Jews' preference for their own beliefs rather than for the new teaching of Jesus and his followers. If so, they do not bear directly on Luke's attitude towards the law but more generally on the question of Jewish–Christian relations. Moreover, because it was generally agreed that old wine was better than new Ber. 51a; Lucian *De Merc. Cond.* 26), it does not follow that Luke favours Judaism or that he is making a reactionary plea. It is rather a statement of fact, which the analogy neither condones nor condemns, and rests upon the commonplace observation that most people prefer old and familiar ways to new ones just as they prefer old wine to new.

In several places, therefore, Luke implicitly or explicitly affirms the validity of the law, especially insofar as it results in practical piety and obedience. He also provides several examples of legal piety, nowhere more so than in the birth narratives. The collection of stories and hymns in Lk. 1–2 is pervaded by an aura of simple, unaffected piety among the parents of Jesus and John and those with whom they came into contact. The constant reference to prayer, prophecy, worship, fasting, visions and angelic messengers expresses a form of piety strongly influenced by Old Testament ideals. Woven into this material are several references to the law, described variously as 'the law of the Lord' (2:23–4, 39), 'the law of Moses' (2:22), 'the custom of the law' (1:27 cf. 24:2) and 'the commandments and ordinances of the Lord' (1:6). We shall consider each of these in turn while recognizing the considerable degree to which they are coloured by their immediate surroundings.

The description of Zechariah and Elizabeth as 'righteous ($\delta i \kappa a \iota o \varsigma$) before God, walking in all the commandments and ordinances ($\dot{e}\nu\tau o\lambda a i$, $\delta \iota \kappa a \iota \omega \mu a \tau a$) of the Lord blameless', is strongly reminiscent of the Old Testament concept of joyful obedience to God's law.[24] Their obedience to the law would be partially fulfilled by Zechariah's priestly duties (1:8) and the description of their piety is doubtless relevant to the situation described in 1:10. Their barrenness, it is implied, is not a punitive condition resulting from their sinfulness (cf. I Sam. 1:5f; 2:5–8), for they are blameless ($\check{a}\mu\epsilon\mu\pi\tau o\varsigma$) and thus join the line of pious yet barren couples for whom God miraculously intervenes (Gen. 17:17; Judges 13:2f; I Sam.

1:1f). The description of their piety, however, stands independently of their immediate circumstances and sets the tone for the birth narratives as a whole.

In 1:59; 2:21 there are passing references to the circumcision of John and Jesus and the associated practice of naming. The former was a legal obligation (Lev. 12:3, etc.) while the latter was probably influenced by a similar Graeco-Roman custom.[25] In neither case, however, is attention drawn specifically to the fulfilment of the law. They are incidental details, predictable within the thoroughly Jewish context of the narratives, and at most contribute towards the overall picture of legal and cultic piety expressed more directly elsewhere.

Lk. 2:22–4 contains a trio of references to legal obedience in connection with the ceremonies of purification and presentation. Both are stated to be part of the law of the Lord or Moses and the appropriate Old Testament text is in each case cited:

> 'And when the time came for their (αὐτῶν) purification according to the law of Moses, they brought him up to Jerusalem to present him to the Lord (as it is written in the law of the Lord, "Every male that opens the womb shall be called holy to the Lord"), and to offer a sacrifice according to what is said in the law of the Lord, "a pair of turtle doves or two young pigeons".'

Despite the specific quotations from Ex. 13:2, 12; Lev. 12:2f, Luke's narrative is not wholly clear. The confusion begins in the MSS variants for αὐτῶν, doubtless influenced both by later dogmatic disputes as well as the conflict with Jewish practice. According to Lev. 12:2f the ceremony of purification was for the sake of the mother and not the child, for she alone was unclean after childbirth – and the MSS which substitute αὐτῆς for αὐτῶν reflect this. But neither this, nor the αὐτοῦ of D can make strong claims to originality.[26] The reference to 'their cleansing' is presumably a loose way of speaking of their visit to the Temple, whose main significance turns out to be the presentation of Jesus. Possibly the Greek notion that both mother and child were made unclean by childbirth has had some influence too. The reference to Ex. 13:2, 12 is also somewhat confusing for it refers to the ceremony of redeeming a firstborn child and not his presentation – a custom for which there is no Old Testament legislation. Perhaps in Palestine, and even more widely, the two ceremonies were combined, but we have no confirmation of this from contemporary sources. It becomes clear as the narrative continues that Luke's primary interest was in the presentation rather than the purification, since the latter is not mentioned again. Lk. 2:27 reinforces this perspective by

referring to Jesus' fulfilment of the law – 'the parents brought in the child
to do to him according to the custom of the law' – and the statement that
'when they had performed everything according to the law of the Lord,
they returned to Galilee' in 2:39 probably also refers mainly to this event,
though it may include the purification.

In connection with these events in the Temple we should observe the
description of Simeon and Anna. Of the former Luke says (2:25), he was
'righteous (δίκαιος) and pious (εὐλαβής), looking for the consolation of
Israel; and the Holy Spirit was on him'. The term εὐλαβής, found only
here in the New Testament, appears to be Luke's expression for the Old
Testament ideal of piety. Indeed, if one understands δίκαιος to refer primarily to human relationships then, in conjunction with εὐλαβής, Simeon
exemplifies precisely that form of piety which Luke elsewhere expresses in
the two love commands (10:25f cf. 11:42). Of Anna the prophetess, who
recognizes and publicizes the special significance of the infant Jesus, it is
said that she 'did not depart from the Temple, worshipping with fasting
and prayer day and night' (2:37). The description does not define her as
part of a special order of Temple widows, though she may later have
become a paradigm of Christian widowhood. The main purpose is to
express the constancy of her piety and worship and, as with Simeon, her
witness to the messiahship of Jesus.

In Lk. 2:42 the action of Jesus' parents in taking him at the age of
twelve to celebrate the passover in Jerusalem is described as κατὰ τὸ ἔθος
τῆς ἑορτῆς (2:42). If this phrase refers to celebration of the passover, then
Jesus' parents would be fulfilling the command in Ex. 34:23f; Dt. 16:16f.
However, 'custom' may refer either to the annual pilgrimage to Jerusalem
(cf. verse 41) or to the habit of taking a twelve-year old to the feast to
prepare him for full participation the following year.[27] In either case the
reference would be to customs that had developed in connection with
passover and not specifically to the law.

The overall impression of Lk. 1–2 is of a pious, godly group who are
positively and sympathetically described. One expression of their piety is
their unquestioning fulfilment of legal and cultic obligations. They are
presented as exemplars of Jewish piety – full of the spirit (1:15, 80;
2:25–7) and divine wisdom (2:40, 47) and joyful in their obedience to the
law. There is not the slightest suggestion of criticism either of the ideal
they pursue or their ability to achieve it. The most striking phrase is the
description of Zechariah and Elizabeth as 'blameless' in their obedience to
God's commands, and the most interesting connection with material outside Lk. 1–2 is the description of Simeon in 2:25 (cf. Lk. 10:25f; 11:42).

But even without this direct link, the birth narratives give an ideal example of that piety which affirms the law expressed elsewhere in Luke's Gospel.

Certainly, not all the references to the law in Lk. 1–2 carry the same weight. Some give the impression of being incidental and explanatory (e.g. 1:59; 2:21) and this is brought out in the two allusions to custom, which explain to the reader why a certain course of action was taken. In other cases emphasis on fulfilment of the law is more laboured and is reinforced by what Luke thought to be the appropriate portions of the Old Testament. It would probably be misleading to see fulfilment of the law as a major theme of the birth narratives; it is rather one element in Luke's conception of the ideal of Jewish piety.

The attitude towards the law expressed in these chapters is that obedience to it by the pious and godly is a sufficient and praiseworthy expression of their commitment to God. To what extent Luke is dependent on sources, possibly of Jewish-Christian origin, is of no immediate relevance.[28] The fact remains that he has included them as the frontispiece to his narrative and that, despite many peculiarities, they concur in important respects with the rest of Luke–Acts.[29] Certainly, with respect to the law, there are connections both of language and substance with the material in the rest of the Gospel. One cannot therefore minimize the significance of Lk. 1–2 because they describe events before the public ministry of Jesus. That it is Jewish piety which Luke describes is inevitable in this context; but for Luke it is the piety itself, one of whose expressions is a life of obedience to God's law, which is significant.

Insofar as Jesus obeys the customs and law in Lk. 1–2 it is at the instigation, and under the watchful eye, of his parents. Elsewhere, however, there are a few hints which suggest that he continued this practice. In Lk. 4:16 Jesus is said to pay his customary visit to the synagogue on the sabbath: εἰσῆλθεν κατὰ τὸ εἰωθὸς αὐτῷ ἐν τῇ ἡμέρᾳ τῶν σαββάτων εἰς τὴν συναγωγήν. Luke alone uses the phrase κατὰ τὸ εἰωθός (cf. Mk 6:2; Matt. 13:54) of Jesus' synagogue worship on the sabbath, although other allusions to this habit are found in Lk. 4:31, 44 (cf. Mk 1:21, 34) and Lk. 13:10. The phrase may refer simply to Jesus' attendance at the synagogue each sabbath, as sanctioned by rabbinic tradition.[30] Since Luke includes a reference to Jesus' attendance at the synagogue and draws attention to the phenomenon in 4:16, we might conclude that he is pointing to Jesus' piety and his faithfulness to traditional customs. This would concur with certain aspects of his teaching and with the infancy narratives. R. Banks suggests that in view of the reference to Jesus' teaching in 4:15 and the use of κατὰ τὸ εἰωθός of Paul's synagogue ministry in Ac. 17:2, the phrase refers to

Jesus' teaching in, rather than his attendance at, the synagogue.[31] He notes that elsewhere in Luke Jesus' attendance at the synagogue is associated either with teaching (4:31, 44) or healing (13:10), suggesting that he viewed it as an opportunity for Jesus to extend his ministry to all Jews. That Jesus used synagogue gatherings to further his own aims seems, from Luke, to be clear, but it is improbable that this is conveyed solely by the phrase κατὰ τὸ εἰωθός. The parallel with Ac. 17:2 is imprecise, since there the reference is explicitly to Paul's preaching, and in context Lk. 4:16 most naturally refers to Jesus' participation in synagogue worship.

The remaining two possible allusions to Jesus' obedience to the law both involve healings. In 17:14 he commands the ten lepers to 'go and show yourselves to the priests' – a command which apparently refers to the fulfilment of the legal requirements expected of those healed of leprosy (Lev. 14:2f). In Lk. 5:14 (cf. Mk 1:44; Matt. 8:4), addressing a healed leper, he says: 'Go and show yourself to the priest and make an offering for your cleansing as Moses commanded, as a witness to them.' The obscure final phrase, εἰς μαρτύριον αὐτοῖς has attracted much attention, since it apparently expresses the reason for fulfilling Mosaic regulations. It is unclear whether αὐτοί are the priests or the people or whether the witness is to or against them. Mark has the same phrase in 6:11 and the Lucan parallel removes one ambiguity by adding a preposition: εἰς μαρτύριον ἐπ᾽ αὐτούς (Lk. 9:5). However, this does not help us to resolve the ambiguity in 5:14. Luke may have understood εἰς μαρτύριον αὐτοῖς positively, altering it in 9:5 by the addition of a preposition; or it may be that 9:5 shows that he understood the similar phrase in 5:14 in a negative fashion too. Many think that both Jesus and Mark used the phrase negatively, in the sense of 'a testimony against Israel',[32] and if Luke is interpreted likewise it has less relevance for the question of law. If for the sake of argument we assume the purpose of the testimony to be positive, it could be understood as 'a proof of Jesus' obedience to the law',[33] rather than, for example, as proof that the leper was healed.[34] This would provide us with at least an incidental reference to Jesus' support for Mosaic regulations and at most a deliberate attempt to prove this to the priests or people.

In the material covered so far Luke reveals a distinctly positive attitude towards the law. When the law is under discussion Luke's overriding concern seems to be with the necessity of doing the law, rather than with theoretical discussions about it. At the same time he offers examples of this positive response to the law both in the birth narratives and in occasional hints about the life of Jesus. The other side of the coin is the occasions when he recalls Jesus' condemnation of his contemporaries for their failure to obey God's commands. It is appropriate to mention this material now, since it does not involve criticism of the law, or any suggestion of its abrogation; rather, it presents the rejection of certain perversities of human behaviour and religiosity. A brief account will suffice, since it is related only indirectly to our theme. Much of the polemic is directed against the scribes and Pharisees and can be summarized as their failure to keep the two commands which, Luke supposes, they agree to be a correct summary of the law. Their attitude to sinners and outcasts (7:36f; 5:29f; 15:1−32), love of money (16:14−15) and religious hypocrisy (12:1−3; 20:45−7) are pilloried, and their piety is unfavourably compared with that shown by those they despise (7:36f; 18:9−14). In addition Lk. 11:37f presents a pessimistic catalogue of their shortcomings: they neglect the central commands of the law (verse 42) and delight in status and public recognition (verse 43); they impose a multitude of legal obligations, yet make no effort to help people fulfil them (verse 46); they murder the prophets and apostles (verses 47−51); and they hide the knowledge of God's will from his people (verse 52).

It is clear that in none of these passages is there polemic against the law itself. Indeed, as we have seen, in at least one saying (verse 42) scribal legislation is viewed positively even though it has been abused. Noteworthy too is their failure to help men fulfil their legal obligations (verse 46). It is not the imposition of the obligations themselves which is condemned, even though they are described as 'burdens hard to bear ($\phi o \rho \tau \acute{\iota} \alpha \ \delta v \sigma \beta \acute{\alpha} \sigma \tau \alpha \kappa \tau \alpha$)', but the failure of the religious leaders to help the people fulfil them. It appears that this, rather than their failure to repeal some of their laws or their knack of finding casuistic evasions of the law's intent,[35] is the meaning of the accusation that they did not lift a finger to ease men's burdens.

Most of the polemical passages in Luke are directed at the religious leaders of Judaism. It is they and not the common people who are in the firing line − a division which shows itself elsewhere too (Lk. 7:24−30; 13:10−17; 19:47−8; 20:6−19). Luke's picture of Jesus' critique of his contemporaries concurs with the material on the law which we have already considered. At the same time as he both emphasizes and illustrates a positive understanding of and obedience to the law, he also provides vivid descriptions of the opposite. The law, so to speak, is independent of those who use it and those who abuse it. It can be the means of expressing profound and genuine piety and it can be ignored and perverted by the very people who claim to know it best.

It is of some interest that in 11:49 Luke mentions 'prophets and apostles' in place of Matthew's 'prophets, wise men and scribes' (Matt. 23:34). The mention of apostles shifts the saying clearly into the Christian era and 'prophets' may include Christian prophets too.[36] Doubtless he was thinking of the persecution of apostles and leaders which he describes in Acts, and therefore understood this pattern of behaviour to extend at least into the apostolic era and probably into his own day too. This might in turn indicate that the inclusion of the polemic against the religious leaders of Judaism was no mere antiquarian gesture, but had contemporary relevance for Luke and his readers — suggesting that they stood at a distance from and experienced the antipathy of Jewish officialdom as they knew it. Although historically we cannot draw a direct line of descent from Pharisaism to rabbinism, even less from Palestinian leaders before 70 C.E. to diaspora leaders after the war, the association would not have been difficult for Luke and his readers.

A different, but equally positive, aspect of the law — when it functions as prophecy — should also be considered as part of Luke's affirmation of the law. The importance of this theme for Luke is well known and need not be rehearsed in detail. The *locus classicus* comes in the post-resurrection period described at the end of the Gospel:

> 24:27: Beginning with Moses and all the prophets, he interpreted to them in all the scriptures the things concerning himself.

> 24:44: These are my words which I spoke to you while I was still with you, that everything written about me in the law of Moses and the prophets and psalms must be fulfilled.

These are the most comprehensive and categorical affirmations in Luke—Acts of the prophetic function of the law. As one part of the scriptures it can, like the other two, be a source of testimonies for the person and work of Jesus — and it is the christological theme which, in these passages at least, predominates. The prophetic function of the law may also be alluded to in the appearance of Moses and Elijah in Lk. 9:29, 32 and in the statement in Lk. 16:16. He returns to this theme more frequently in Acts but even there the relative paucity of references belies its significance. This is not for Luke mere repetition of a standard Christian conviction, for the scheme of promise and fulfilment lies at the heart of his historical and theological understanding. Events past, present and future are comprehended in this scheme and it expresses a profound conviction about divine control and order.[37] Despite the sweeping claim made in 24:27, 44, Luke nowhere in the Gospel and only rarely in Acts provides specific quotation from the law in its prophetic function. He makes more use of the prophets and writings, and even then some events — the death of Jesus for example — are difficult to relate to specific passages. Even if we are left short of examples, however, there can be no doubt about Luke's overall perspective.

A further curiosity is that the prophetic function of the law is asserted
in complete isolation from what we might call its prescriptive function.
There is no attempt to correlate the two even when the prescriptive function is viewed positively. Luke, of course, is not alone in this, for the same
can be said of most early Christian writers. Whether they take a positive or
negative view of the prescriptions of the law, they seem content to place
this side by side with its prophetic function without systematic reflection.

B. Challenging the law?

Within this general category two strands of evidence need to be discussed:
sayings which appear to supplement the law or extend its demands, and
those which abrogate or alter the demands of the law either directly or by
implication. It could be argued that the first group form a distinct
category, but the relevant material is slight and, although it contains no
explicit criticism of the law and in one instance directly affirms it, distinctively Christian teaching is placed on a par with the law. The law is
thus necessarily relegated from the position of exclusive arbiter of man's
relationship to God, and the new element which is brought into play –
the teaching of Jesus – leads us naturally into a consideration of his criticism of the law.

The most appropriate place to start is the discussion with the rich
young ruler (Lk. 18:18–23; Mk 10:17–22; Matt. 19:16–22). The differences from the Markan account are mostly stylistic, though a few may be
more significant. The man is identified as a ruler (ἄρχων), a characteristically Lucan term (Lk. 8:41; 12:58; 14:1; 23:13, 25; 24:20, cf. Acts 3:17;
4:5, 8, 26; 13:27; Matt. 9:18, 23, 20:25). Usually these rulers are cast
as enemies of Jesus and his followers, and it may be for this reason that
Luke does not have Mark's statement that Jesus 'loved him' (Mk 10:21).
The addition of πάντα in the command to sell possessions and give to the
poor (Lk. 18:22) intensifies the demand and recalls the frequent occasions
when Luke broaches the subject of wealth.

Approaching Jesus with the words 'good teacher' the ruler is rebuked
by the observation that 'no-one is good but God alone'. This sharp and
curious response Matthew apparently found embarrassing and he gives a
different version of both question and answer. Luke, however, concurs
with Mark and presumably took Jesus' observation at its face value to
mean 'ethically good' or perhaps 'gracious'.[38] The effect is to turn attention away from Jesus to God and it is the commands of God which Jesus
immediately recalls rather than new teaching of his own. The logic of the
exchange might seem to imply that since God alone is good he alone can

give commands, though as the discussion continues Jesus' own demands come to the fore. The selection of commands from the decalogue is unusual in that this particular combination — Mark includes a command against fraud and Matthew the command to love one's neighbour — is not found elsewhere. The practice of quoting the socio-ethical commands of the decalogue either verbally or in substance is, however, not uncommon in Judaism and early Christianity where they often serve as a convenient summary of the law.[39] In reply to the ruler's request for the key to eternal life Jesus' immediate response is thus to point to the central commands of the law. Whether the discussion would have ended there if the ruler had not claimed to have observed them, as it does in the similar situation in Lk. 10:25–8, we cannot say. The force of his claim is not clear. Perhaps it is confined to the commands listed, the fulfilment of which would have been relatively uncomplicated; but if Luke and his readers knew that lists such as these were a shorthand way of referring to the law as a whole, his claim would be seen to be much more comprehensive.

That the ruler had observed the commands specifically mentioned is not contested but, says Jesus, he lacks one thing: 'Sell all that you own and distribute it to the poor, and you will have treasure in heaven; then come, follow me' (verse 23). What began as an apparently straightforward answer to his question in terms of the demands of the law now takes a significantly different turn. In what some consider to be a Christian addition to the original pericope,[40] gaining eternal life is seen to depend not merely on obedience to the law but also on two further demands of Jesus: radical divestment of wealth and Christian discipleship. Indeed Luke sees them not as two demands but two intimately related aspects of the same demand. This is indicated not only by the words of verse 22 — 'One thing you still lack' — and by the confirmation of the theme of 'following Jesus' in verses 28–30, but also by the connection of the themes of conversion and the use of wealth both in Jewish writings (Test. Job 15:8; 4:6f; Jos. and Asen. 55:14)[41] and elsewhere in Luke–Acts (Lk. 19:1–10; Ac. 10:2, 30–2). Moreover, the obligation of almsgiving and the notion that it would bring heavenly reward are common Jewish themes quite apart from the context of conversion (Tob. 4:9; Ps. Sol. 9:5; IV Ezr. 6:5; 7:7; Sir. 16:14).

An ambivalent attitude towards the law is expressed in this incident. On the one hand the law's commands are quoted approvingly as a guide for those who wish to inherit eternal life; yet on the other hand it is clearly implied that the law has been supplemented by the teaching of Jesus. Care for the poor could have been seen as a fulfilment of the law, but the call for radical poverty and personal discipleship could not. The demands of

the law are not abrogated but they are supplemented. The contrast with
Lk. 10:25–8 is noteworthy. The two passages are linked not only by a
similar concern for the law but, in Luke especially, by an identical opening
question – 'What shall I do to inherit eternal life?' – asked in both cases
by a Jewish leader. The reader is thus encouraged to compare the two
stories. In the first Jesus commends the lawyer's summary of the law in
the two love commands and declares that obedience to them will result in
eternal life. In the second a quite different summary of the law is given by
Jesus himself and immediately followed by supplementary demands. Common to both is a positive attitude towards the law, but peculiar to the
second is the implication that obedience to the commands of the law alone
is no guarantee of eternal life. And if we follow up Luke's hint and
attempt to interpret the one in terms of the other we meet with little
success. It is conceivable that the distribution of wealth fulfils the command to love one's neighbour, but it is not the most natural thing to
identify the call to follow Jesus with the command to love God.[42] Thus
these very similar stories seem to be in tension with each other, at least
with respect to the law – a tension which, incidentally, is less evident in
the Markan parallels. In one the law is sufficient in itself, in the other it is
not.

Closely related to 18:18f, in its emphasis upon the significance of the
teaching of Jesus which supplements the law, is the sermon on the plain
(Lk. 6:20–49). We can leave aside the complex issue of the relationship to
Matt. 5–7, and make do with two interrelated observations. First, the
concluding section of the sermon in both Luke and Matthew (Lk. 6:49–9;
Matt. 7:24–7) emphasizes the importance of the preceding words of
Jesus: whoever listens to and acts upon them builds on an unshakeable
foundation. Unlike Matt. 5–7, secondly, Luke's version of the sermon
contains neither the antitheses (Matt. 5:21f) nor any overt discussion of
the law (Matt. 5:17–20). Much of the teaching is essentially the same, but
in Luke there is no explicit contrast with Jewish legal teaching. Thus,
while the substance of several of Matthew's antitheses is missing altogether
in Luke, it is significant that in the parallel in Lk. 6:27f there is no explicit
contrast with the *lex talionis*. Taking these two observations together,
while no specific contrast is drawn between the teaching of Jesus and the
teaching of the law, yet for the former a singular and crucial function is
claimed. To follow it is to build on a sure foundation, which is simply
another way of speaking about the gaining of eternal life. In its assertion
that obedience to the teaching of Jesus provides the ultimate guarantee of
eternal life it comes close to the implicit claim of 18:18f.

At this point an influential interpretation of Lk. 16:16–17, which would place it firmly in this category, deserves mention. H. Conzelmann, for whom 16:16 is an essential clue to Lucan theology, not unreasonably interprets the reference to the law in 16:16*a* in terms of the verse which immediately follows: while it might seem that 'the preaching of the kingdom' has superseded 'the law and the prophets', in view of 16:17 this cannot have been Luke's meaning. 'To the traditional verse Lk. 16:16 there is immediately added the obviously editorial statement of v. 17. Thus even if the original sense of this verse pointed to a break, to the supersession of the old aeon by the new, Luke makes it point at the same time to a continuity: until now there was "only" the law and the prophets, but from now on there is "also" the preaching of the kingdom.'[43] In this context the function of the law and the prophets was to call for repentance, a role they can still perform in the new era when the kingdom is preached. This understanding of verses 16–17 puts some strain on Conzelmann's tripartite division of Lucan salvation-history, but his exegesis of 16:16 with respect to the law can be considered independently. If it is correct – and we shall consider the alternatives later – it provides additional evidence for the category under consideration: the law, understood in a particular way, continues to be valid in the Christian era; but in addition there is now the message of the kingdom preached by Jesus and his followers. The law is affirmed, but also supplemented.

A closely related verse is the obvious starting point for an investigation of the material which presents a more radical challenge to Mosaic authority and the law: 'Everyone who divorces his wife and marries another commits adultery, and he who marries a woman divorced from her husband commits adultery' (Lk. 16:18). The condemnation of the remarriage of divorcees, couched in terms which apparently imply the condemnation of divorce as well, contradicts the Mosaic provisions of Dt. 24:1f and bypasses scribal disputes over the proper grounds for divorce. The Mosaic law does not, of course, command divorce and both the Old Testament (Prov. 5:15f; Mal. 2:14–16) and rabbinic tradition (Git. 90*b*) can view it with some distaste. Nevertheless, since the law outlines the proper procedures for divorce it was natural to conclude that divorce was sanctioned by Moses. This is the view of rabbinic authorities and their debates concern the proper grounds for divorce and not the legitimacy of divorce as such (cf. too Jos. *Ant.* XV.259). Lk. 16:18, therefore, challenges Mosaic authority and current Jewish practice, and it is difficult to think that Luke was unaware of this even though he does not explicitly draw it to our attention. If Mark was one of his sources, then although he omits the discussion in Mk 10:2f he must have seen the implications of Lk. 16:18. That it consists of increasing rather than relaxing the demands of the law should not be allowed to obscure the directness of Jesus' challenge – although we shall consider this matter more fully at a later stage.

Luke records four disputes over the sabbath law, of which two are shared with the other synoptic Gospels (Lk. 6:1–5, 6–11; Mk 2:23–8; 3:1–6; Matt. 12:1–8, 9–14) and two are in Luke alone (Lk. 13:10–17; 14:1–6). The first deals with the picking of corn by the disciples and the other three with healings performed by Jesus. In terms of content Lk. 6:1–5 is the most significant and, because it is the first, sets the tone for the interpretation of the other three.

Lk. 6:1 opens with a curious variant reading. Following the opening phrase Ἐγένετο δὲ ἐν σαββάτῳ, many manuscripts add the word δευτεροπρώτῳ. The significance of this hybrid term is difficult to surmise though, as the indisputably *lectio difficilior*, it is commonly taken to be the original reading. There are various explanations, none wholly satisfactory, and those which attempt to relate it to the substance of the dispute are the least convincing. Thus a connection with Lev. 23:15, which is itself ambiguous, but which appears to forbid the eating of corn on a particular sabbath,[44] is unlikely to have been in the mind of Luke or his readers; and even if it was it would do no more than sharpen a conflict which is already present. It is perhaps best explained either as a reference to the 'second sabbath after the first', in which the 'first' (following Markan chronology) is 4:31 and 4:16 is overlooked, or as the conflation of two separate readings based on different calculations. Thus one scribe wrote 'first' with reference to 6:6f and another wrote 'second' with reference to 4:31, while a third later combined the two.[45] The reference to Abiathar is missing from Luke and Matthew and was probably intended to correct a historical error. It is, however, one of several ways in which Matthew and Luke agree against Mark which are sufficient to give some credibility to the suggestion that they follow a non-Markan source;[46] but for our purposes they are significant only insofar as they alter the sense of the passage. Comparing Luke and Mark, it seems that most of the differences are stylistic variations which have little bearing on the overall meaning. The absence of Mark's ὅτε χρείαν ἔσχεν, if one sees it as an allusion to the rabbinic justification of the action of David and his companions on the grounds of severe hunger which threatened life,[47] might indicate that Matthew and Luke wish to exclude a line of argument which undermines Jesus' choice of an example. But without further indications this must remain improbable. The absence of Mk 2:27 is not so readily explained and calls for comment below.

The inclusion of a reference to rubbing corn in the hands (ψώχοντες ταῖς χερσίν) in Luke 6:1 could be intended to clarify the cause of the dispute which in Mark is not clear. There is no suggestion that the disciples had exceeded sabbath travel limits and plucking another's corn was allowed in the law (Dt. 23:4–5 cf. Lev. 19:9–10; 23:22). The law forbids all work on the sabbath (Ex. 31:14–15; 34:21, etc.), a broad proscription which inevitably requires further definition of the term 'work'. The earliest systematic interpretations of the command are found in Jub. 2:17–33, CD 10:14–11:18, and these were later expanded by the rabbis into precise and detailed commands which eventually became the subject of three tractates of the Mishnah (Shabbat, Erubin, Beza). In Shab. 7:2 the third of the thirty-nine forbidden actions is reaping and this would appear to be the point of the dispute in Mark. Maybe Luke, or the tradition he follows, thought it necessary to emphasize this by adding a reference to rubbing the corn by hand.

In all three accounts it is the disciples who pick the corn but, even in Luke where the Pharisees' question is addressed to the disciples rather than to Jesus, it is he who assumes responsibility for their action. This illustrates the responsibilities of a teacher for his disciples,[48] but also prepares for the analogy of David's appropriation of the shewbread for himself and his followers.

There are a number of intriguing discussions in rabbinic literature which may have some bearing on the significance of this incident for Jesus and, more certainly, for Matthew, but it is doubtful that they contribute much to Luke's understanding of it. The Old Testament analogy used to justify the action of Jesus and his disciples (Lk. 6:3–4; I Sam. 21:1–6) was inevitably the cause of some embarrassment to rabbinic commentators. The common solution was to justify the action on the grounds of extreme hunger which threatened their lives.[49] This in turn was based on the general principle that the sabbath could be broken if life was endangered (cf. I Macc. 2:29–41)[50] – and it is solely in this context that the famous rabbinic saying on the sabbath must be understood: 'The sabbath is delivered to you, not you to the sabbath' (Mek. Ex. 134; Yom. 85*b*). That Luke understood this to be Jesus' line of argument seems quite improbable.[51] None of the Gospels suggests that the disciples were in dire need, and Luke lacks the Markan phrase – 'when he was in need' – which comes closest to recalling the rabbinic explanation, even though that is probably not its intention. It is equally improbable that the assumption that David's action took place on the sabbath, which is developed by some rabbinic writers (cf. I Sam. 21:2–6; Lev. 24:8–9; Men. 95:6; Yalkut on I Sam. 21:5), has informed Luke's interpretation of the incident,[52] for when the analogy is quoted no reference is made to the sabbath. Indeed, the analogy is imprecise in more than one way: not only is there no allusion to the sabbath in David's action but, whereas his error was to eat forbidden food, the disciples' error was to work on a forbidden day. It would seem therefore that the analogy rests solely on the fact that both were examples of illegal action. It is improbable that a rabbinic line of argument is being pursued for not only is the particular example one which the rabbis explained as an exception, but the argument from haggadah to halakah would probably not have produced a legally acceptable rabbinic conclusion.[53]

If such arguments appear to shed little light on Luke's account, attempts to find a contrast between the moral and ritual law — of the sort that suggest 'the needs of men are more important than ritual laws'[54] — are of even less value. They can only be read into and not out of the text. The use of an example involving David and his followers is perhaps not wholly fortuitous in an incident which involves both Jesus and his disciples, but Luke's conclusion (6:5) indicates that it is the analogy between the two leaders which is most significant. What each does in relation to his followers is incidental and, in any case, not identical. In the one case the followers act and the leader justifies them, while in the other the leader acts and the followers tag along. But Luke does not stop at a simple one to one analogy between two leaders or two illegal acts. For if we take his conclusion to the story in 6:5 (= Mk 2:28), which is not preceded by a version of Mk 2:27, as the key to his understanding, it seems clear that he also wishes to make a broader christological point.

The point is not, it would seem, that Jesus is the 'son of David' or, more precisely, that the Son of Man is to be identified with the son of David. It is simpler and more apposite: 'The Son of Man is lord of the sabbath.' As lord of the sabbath he stands above the law and implicitly claims the right to define it.[55] But although the christological conclusion is primary it is not enunciated *in vacuo*. The practical consequences are quite clear: both Jesus and his disciples were free to act in opposition to the current interpretation of sabbath law. It is the Son of Man who decides what is and what is not acceptable behaviour on the sabbath. In this connection it is important to observe that the charge of illegality in 6:2 — 'Why do they do that which is unlawful (οὐκ ἔξεστιν) to do on the sabbath' — is not denied or disputed. Indeed, the example of David confirms it by echoing the charge, since he eats 'that which it is not lawful (οὐκ ἔξεστιν) except for the priests alone to eat'. The repetition of οὐκ ἔξεστιν and the fact that it is precisely the element of illegality which binds the two incidents together, confirm that evasion of the charge of illegality is not intended, at least in the terms in which Jesus' opponents pose it. Whatever other ramifications there may be in the assertion that

Jesus is lord of the sabbath, one remains clear: it can be used to justify a rejection of current sabbath practice.

It might be argued that the implicit critique of the sabbath is blunted by the reference to an Old Testament analogy. Indeed some think these verses were added later in order to tone down Jesus' response by indicating Old Testament precedents for illegal behaviour,[56] a point which Matthew reinforces by adding an example of sabbath breaking which was familiar and acceptable to rabbinic thinking (Matt. 12:5–6; Shab. 132*b*; Pes. 6:1). But even in Matthew there is only a half-hearted use of the rabbinic mode of argument, for if he knew that these were rabbinic examples he would presumably also have known that the rabbis treated them strictly as exceptions. Any attempt to draw general conclusions from them would have cut no ice with rabbinic opponents, unless in Matthew's day the rabbinic explanation of them had not been formulated. Above all, however, Matthew uses the examples as the prelude to a christological point – 'that something greater than the Temple is here' (verse 6*b*). Whether the allusion to I Sam. 21 goes back to Jesus[57] or to a later stage in the tradition, and whatever its original purpose, in Luke it can hardly be said to reduce the force of Jesus' words. In fact its effect is precisely the opposite, for it emphasizes the illegality of the act, offers no extenuating explanations and leads to the radical conclusion that Jesus is lord of the sabbath.

The absence of an equivalent to Mk 2:27 – 'The sabbath was made for man and not man for the sabbath' – in Luke and Matthew has elicited a variety of explanations, which depend largely on how the relationship between 2:27 and 2:28 is understood. That Mk 2:28 was originally a saying about 'man' rather than the 'Son of Man' is a conjecture which makes sense of the conjunction of the two verses in Mk 2:27–8.[58] It is clear, however, that Luke received it as a 'Son of Man' saying and the absence of an equivalent to Mk 2:27 may be because he could not see the connection with the 'Son of Man' saying. Alternatively he may have feared that the words were open to misinterpretation either by those who wished to abandon the law altogether,[59] or by those who wished to retain full sabbath observance in Christian circles,[60] although the former explanation scarcely concurs with the radical implications of the Lucan narrative as it stands and the latter would require further proof that Judaizing Christians were a problem for Luke. Perhaps the simplest explanation for the absence of 2:27 is that it allows all our attention to be focussed on the bold christological assertion which follows. The conjunction of a saying about man with one about the Son of Man to some extent distracts our attention from the latter.[61] Thus neither the absence of Mk 2:27 nor the presence of the analogy with David effectively tempers the radical claim made by Jesus. Certainly, Luke wishes to emphasize the christological conclusion but, with respect to the sabbath law, the implications of this claim are no less challenging than those contained in Mk 2:27. For an unambiguous example of the modification of Jesus' words one need look no further than the variant, almost certainly secondary, reading in Lk. 6:5 (D, Marcion).[62]

The whole account in Lk. 6:1–5 is somewhat cryptic. The accusation against the disciples is only indirectly answered in verses 3–4 and it implies not so much a protest against, as an acceptance of, the charge. The assertion of verse 5 seems only loosely appended to verses 3–4, though some see them related as conclusion to premise.[63] The general drift, however, seems clear. The disciples disobey the sabbath law and Jesus defends their action by allusion to the Old Testament and, above all, by a claim to personal authority which implicitly gives him the right to make or break sabbath commands.

We cannot be certain precisely what conclusions Luke drew from Lk. 6:1–5 with respect to the attitude of Jesus and his followers towards the law. It might be argued that, since the sabbath institution itself is not overtly challenged, the dispute hangs merely on scribal definitions of the law. Since scribal casuistry and not the law itself is challenged, Jesus' followers remain under obligation to sabbath law, albeit with a new freedom. Technically this may be true, but it rests on a distinction which Luke nowhere uses, least of all in this passage, and which would have been unthinkable to many of his Jewish contemporaries and possibly Jewish-Christians too. Luke nowhere makes the distinction between law and tradition, such as we find in Mk 7:1f; 10:2f, and the Pharisees' initial assessment of the situation in 6:1 is not disputed because it rests on mere tradition or, indeed, on any other legal grounds. As he presents the story, the disciples openly break the sabbath law and Jesus defends their action, a defence based ultimately on a self-affirmation which brings an entirely new element into consideration. The claim to lordship over the sabbath ultimately subordinates the sabbath to Jesus and does not merely establish him as the arbiter of sabbath disputes. If the sabbath is subordinate to Jesus so is the law. It is because Luke seems more anxious to make a christological point than to draw out its practical implications that we have some difficulty defining the latter, and this may also suggest that the issue of sabbath observance was of no immediate concern to Luke or his readers.

Further glimpses of how Luke viewed the sabbath are to be found in the disputes over sabbath healing. There are a few distinctive elements in

Luke's account of the healing of the man with a withered hand (Lk. 6:6–11; cf. Mk 3:1–6; Matt. 12:9–14). The incident occurs on a different sabbath from 6:1–5 (ἐν ἑτέρῳ σαββάτῳ verse 6) and Jesus is credited with a clairvoyant talent (verse 8 cf. Lk. 5:22). The antagonists are again specified as 'scribes and Pharisees', and this brings to a climax Luke's series of controversies between Jesus and these two groups (Lk. 5:1–6, 11). There is no reference to Jesus' anger and grief at their hardness of heart (Mk 3:5) and the conclusion is altered by an allusion to the anger of the opponents and the omission of any reference to the Herodians or the plan to kill Jesus (verse 11). None of these, however, essentially alters the story as told in Mark. The dispute over the sabbath remains and is summarized in verse 9: 'I ask you, is it lawful to do good (ἀγαθοποιῆσαι) on the sabbath or do harm (κακοποιῆσαι), to save life (σῶσαι) or to destroy it (ἀπολέσαι)?' The rabbinic view that healing on the sabbath was justified only if life was endangered[64] was apparently known in the first century. Jesus' statement goes beyond the issue of healing and asserts implicitly the legality of 'doing good' and 'saving life'. The second principle might have been an acceptable expression of rabbinic law, though it would scarcely have been applicable in the immediate situation where there was no danger to life. The first principle, however, would have appeared far too broad to be an acceptable understanding of the law, and could have been interpreted as implying a radical modification of sabbath commands, since it sets the requirement to do good above the requirement to rest in such a way that if the two conflict the former takes precedence.

It is doubtful that Luke drew this conclusion. His intention seems to have been to illustrate the character of Jesus' mission[65] and the nature of his opponents rather than to reflect upon the legal implications of Jesus' words. In this respect it concurs with the previous pericope (6:1–5) and is perhaps best illustrated by 13:10–17; 14:1–6, narratives which are found only in Luke. The healing of a man with dropsy occurs during a meal with a Pharisee. On this occasion Jesus raises the issue himself and, unlike 6:6–11, directly in terms of healing: 'Is it lawful to heal on the sabbath, or not?' The Pharisees are curiously silent (verse 4) and remain so throughout the incident. Jesus draws an analogy with the rescue of an ass[66] or ox from a well (verse 5 cf. Matt. 12:11) and his opponents apparently could not reply (verse 6). The reason for their silence, according to Luke at least, was probably that they recognized the force of Jesus' argument from common practice. Rabbinic legislation on such matters[67] is mostly later than the first century, though doubtless similar debates took place at an earlier time (cf. CD 11:13–17). Perhaps in the first century rescuing an animal met with Pharisaic and rabbinic approval – if only negatively by their failure to proscribe it — though later legislation allowed no more than the feeding and watering of distressed animals (Shab. 128*b*). The connection between the analogy and the healing is not spelled out, probably because of its proximity to the similar story in 13:10–17. We already know from that story and from 6:6–11 that the Pharisees disapproved of sabbath healing, so we must assume that Luke intends Jesus' action to be seen as a contradiction of current sabbath law which would not have met with Pharisaic approval.

In the closely related incident (Lk. 13:10–17) the leader of the synagogue (ἀρχισυνάγωγος), indignant that Jesus has healed a crippled woman, summarizes the Pharisaic–scribal objection: 'There are six days on which work ought to be done; come on those days and be healed, and not on the sabbath day' (verse 14). Jesus instantly replies with a charge of hypocrisy and again uses an analogy with the sabbath treatment of animals — the untying and watering of oxen and asses. Later rabbinic law allowed these actions on the sabbath,[68] but here, as in 14:5 and Matt. 12:11, the reference may be to common custom rather than scribal legislation.[69] Analogy and healing are closely connected. If the unbinding of an animal is allowed on the sabbath how much more should the unbinding of a woman be allowed on the sabbath — the woman's infirmity being ascribed to the 'binding of Satan' (verses 15–16). The sabbath is thus declared to be the day for healing *par excellence*, a claim which operates on a different level from, and ultimately contradicts, rabbinic thinking. Jesus does not argue, as sages frequently do, about the legitimacy of certain exceptions to the sabbath command but views the sabbath in a totally different light as the most appropriate day on which to do good and save life (6:9). The purpose of the sabbath is not to forbid works of compassion but to encourage them.

An understanding of Luke's presentation of the sabbath disputes requires some knowledge of the role of the sabbath in first-century Judaism. As one of the most clearly visible signs of Jewish allegiance, sabbath observance became one of the hallmarks of Judaism in the Hellenistic era. It was one of the features most frequently noted by pagan writers, often for the purpose of ridicule (Juv. *Sat.* 14:95f; Seneca, quoted by Augustine, *Civ. Dei* VI.10–11), while for Jewish writers it was a mark of great distinction and they were quick to point out that even non-Jews copied their sabbath customs (Jos. *Ap.* II.282; cf. Suet. *Tiberius* 32). As emphasis upon the significance of the law increased so did scrupulous observance of the sabbath, to the point where it could be seen as the very heart of the law.[70] The comprehensive prohibition of work cried out for exposition and early attempts to define it (Jub. 2:17–23; 50:6–13; CD

10:11—11:18) are probably a fairly accurate picture of first-century practice at least among certain groups. The more extensive codifications found in rabbinic literature, which may include some material from the first century, show the seriousness with which the sabbath command was taken. The first Christians appear to have kept the sabbath, though how far this was true of Gentile Churches is not clear (cf. Col. 2:16; Rom. 14:5f; Gal. 4:10). Sunday worship seems to have been an early innovation (I Cor. 16:2; Ac. 20:7) although it is only towards the end of the first century and beyond that we have clear signs of the substitution of Sunday for sabbath (Barn. 15:9; Did. 14:1; Ign. *Magn.* 9:1; Just. *Apol.* I.67.3). Among some Christians, however, observance of the sabbath lingered on.[71]

The broad outlines are thus clear and would provoke little disagreement. From the evidence available, however, answers to more precise questions, such as would help us to locate Luke's view of the sabbath more precisely, are not forthcoming. We do not know, for example, how detailed scribal legislation was in the first century, and there is a sizeable gulf between the early systematization of sabbath law and the later discussions of the rabbis. The transition from the one to the other is difficult to date and both sets of evidence may at any rate tell us more about the sabbath customs of special groups (Qumran monastics, rabbinic scholars) than about sabbath observance among Jews as a whole. Likewise, it is unclear whether sabbath practices in the diaspora were different from those in Palestine, possibly even differing from city to city, or whether there was a basic uniformity among all Jews. We can be fairly certain that most Jews took the sabbath command seriously, but there is no evidence to tell us how it was understood in different times and places. The transition from sabbath to Sunday is also obscure and among Jewish-Christians who continued to observe the sabbath it is not clear how, if at all, their new faith affected this practice.

It would appear that Luke was more interested in the christological than in the legal implications of the sabbath stories. Jesus' actions and words are presented above all as an indication of his status and an illustration of the character of his ministry.[72] His decision to heal on the sabbath is defended by a new assessment of its purpose which rests not on an appeal to the ordinances of creation against those of Torah[73] — for no such appeal is made — but ultimately on his own judgement. His claim to be lord of the sabbath in 6:5 epitomizes his attitude in all the sabbath disputes, and there is no serious attempt to engage Judaism on its own terms, despite the allusion to I Samuel 21 (Lk. 6:3—4) and accepted custom (Lk. 13:15; 14:5).[74] Ultimately the debates do not turn on disputed points of sabbath halakah and, in 6:1—5 especially, no attempt is made to deny the illegality of Jesus' behaviour as defined by his opponents. This is precisely because for Luke the essential issue is not the sabbath law *per se* but the person and work of Jesus. He shows little interest in the practical ramifications for sabbath observance among Christians. This may be because it was not a live issue for him or for his readers, which in turn suggests that they were Gentile Christians for whom sabbath observance was of no consequence.

Having said this, however, we can still consider the kind of conclusions a reader of Luke's Gospel might have drawn about sabbath practice. This may not be Luke's main interest, but we cannot ignore the fact that the christological assertions arise out of practical situations, nor can we suppose that Luke was unaware of the significance of sabbath observance in first-century Judaism. It might be argued, for example, that the disputes are primarily with the religious leaders, that none of them overtly set aside the sabbath as an institution of Torah, and that the proposal is merely for a new understanding of its purpose. Certainly, even in Luke's account, there is no sweeping rejection of sabbath observance but, while some of the conflicts rest on fine points of sabbath law which may have been as open to dispute in Luke's day as they probably were in Jesus', Pharisaic—rabbinic debate is on the whole by-passed and a new set of principles introduced — the use of the sabbath to do good, to save life and to heal. On a formal level there are similarities between Jesus' line of argument and current Jewish debates, but they are superficial. Even when we allow for the limitations of our information, both the content and the consequences of Jesus' statements would appear to run counter to both current Jewish belief and practice. Lk. 6:1–5 goes further still and lifts the discussion onto a quite different, and distinctively Christian, plane. Not only is the sabbath to be seen as a time to encourage rather than constrain works of compassion, but even rules about sabbath work are no longer in force — for corn-picking can scarcely be described as a work of compassion. More important still, the sabbath institution as such is subordinated to its lord, the Son of Man. Taken to its logical conclusion this christological claim mounts a fundamental challenge to the sabbath and ultimately to the law itself. That a radical conclusion such as this can be drawn, even though Luke shows no inclination to do so, remains significant.

There are a few more passages which might be understood to promote criticism of the law. Lk. 9:59–60 (cf. Matt. 8:21–2) reads: 'To another he said, "Follow me". But he said, "Lord, let me first go and bury my father." But he said to him, "Leave the dead to bury their own dead; but as for you, go and proclaim the kingdom of God." ' This startling statement challenges not only the command to honour one's parents but also a sacred custom which every Jew held dear (Gen. 25:9; Tob. 4:3; 6:14;

Aboth 1:2; Ber. 3:1*a*) and which in some cases was believed to take pre-
cedence over all their duties (Ber. 3:1). Certainly, it is to be connected
with similar demands which elevate discipleship over familial obligations
(Lk. 8:19–21; 12:51–3; 14:23–7, etc.), which in turn reflect the apoca-
lyptic theme of the disintegration of families in the last days (Mich. 7:6;
I En. 99:5, 100:1f) and the eschatological urgency of Jesus' mission.[75]
But while this may explain Jesus' command it does not reduce its force.
Even if it is a purely metaphorical way of speaking without practical implications – an unlikely suggestion[76] – legal obligation is still ultimately subordinated to the demands of discipleship. Again, Luke shows no awareness
of the legal implications of this passage, but it remains significant that they
are there to be drawn.

Four other incidents describe a conflict between Jesus and the Pharisees
which may have some bearing on the law (5:17–26, 27–32, 33–5;
11:37–41). The question of fasting (Lk. 5:33–5; Mk 2:18–22; Matt.
9:14–17) can be passed over briefly. The parable of the bridegroom
suggests that Jesus' disciples need not fast while he is present, while the
law required that Jews fast once a year on the day of atonement. It seems
improbable that Jesus' words are intended to discourage participation in
this annual rite and the Gospel writers do not present them in this way.
The contrast is specifically with the weekly fasting of the disciples of John
and the Pharisees and not with the annual fast required of all Jews.

Lk. 5:17–26 (Mk 2:1–12; Matt. 9:1–8) records a dispute over the
healing and forgiveness of a paralytic. In the opening words Luke characteristically adds a reference to the Pharisees and 'teachers of the law'
(νομοδιδάσκαλοι), while in Mark and Matthew they are identified as
'scribes' only half way through the account. The term νομοδιδάσκαλος
occurs only in Luke and the Pastorals (Ac. 5:34; I Tim. 1:7). In this passage it appears to be equivalent to γραμματεύς (cf. verses 17, 21) and may
have been a term current in Luke's day to describe the authoritative
teachers of Judaism. Luke implies that a considerable number gathered to
dispute with Jesus – they came 'from every village of Galilee and Judea
and from Jerusalem' – and thus sets the scene for the series of controversies which follow (5:17–6:11). The heart of the dispute comes in verses
20–1, the question of the power and right to forgive sins. When Jesus
declares the man's sins forgiven he is accused of blasphemy (βλασφημία),
on the grounds that God alone can forgive. Although there is no legal
ruling on this point it is clear that the Old Testament assumes that God
alone can forgive (Ex. 34:6f; Is. 43:25f; 44:2, etc.) and such authority,
for example, is never predicated of the Messiah.[77] As the Son of Man,
Jesus claims the power to forgive sins on earth (verse 24 cf. Lk. 7:47;

24:47; Ac. 2:38; 10:43), an assertion which functions in similar fashion to the claim made in Lk. 6:5.

There is no discussion of the law for it is the prerogative of God rather than the authority of the law which is at stake, but the charge of blasphemy brings the dispute into a legal context. In the LXX blasphemy against God is variously described and is seen as characteristic of Gentiles (Is. 66:3; I Macc. 2:6; II Macc. 8:4; 10:34f; Tob. 1:18). Josephus uses it of attacks on God's people (*Ap.* I.59, 223) and on Moses and the law (*Ant.* III.307; *Ap.* II.143). The rabbis also define blasphemy in a variety of ways: it could refer to those who spoke against the Torah (cf. Ac. 6:11), idolaters, or more narrowly of those who misused the name of God (Sanh. 7:5).[78] Thus while the legal aspects are not pursued in the Gospels, it was potentially a legal matter. The objection of the Pharisees is, from a Jewish viewpoint, quite reasonable, and their charge of blasphemy not merely a loose imprecation. Jesus' claim is not presented as a challenge to the law, but in its challenge to one aspect of current belief it was open to the charge of disobedience to the law — even though the charges are not pressed. The christological affirmation at the heart of the story, like that of Lk. 6:5, implicitly subordinates traditional institutions and teaching to the proclamation of Jesus. It is this above all which Luke wishes to convey, but the legal issues always hover in the background.

Immediately following comes the dispute over Jesus' willingness to eat with the newly converted Levi and his guests (Lk. 5:29f; Mk 2:13–17; Matt. 9:9–13). The crux of the issue is expressed in the concluding verses (verses 30–3): 'And the Pharisees and their scribes murmured against his disciples, saying "Why do you eat and drink with tax collectors and sinners?" And Jesus answered them, "Those who are well have no need of a physician, but those who are sick; I have not come to call the righteous, but sinners to repentance." ' The Pharisees' query springs from their rigorous observance of the rules of purity and tithing. These rules, originally devised in conjunction with the Temple cult, were believed by the Pharisees to be applicable to all Jews in their everyday lives. They observed them scrupulously and hoped ultimately to encourage all Jews to do the same.[79] They had only limited success in the first century and this led them to view those who failed to comply as 'unclean' or 'sinners'. They were thus not only excluded from eating with Gentiles but from eating with most of their fellow Jews too. Mixing with sinners could lead to ceremonial uncleanness and sin by association, and meals were a particular problem for the food could be both unclean and untithed.[80] Jesus followed exactly the opposite course. He regularly consorted with the outcasts and sinners for the purpose, as Luke characteristically adds, of calling them 'to repentance' (εἰς μετάνοιαν).[81] His attitude towards the law in behaving so has been variously assessed. The separatist programme of the Pharisees could be based on the law (Lev. 10:10, etc.) and the Pharisees claimed that it was so. Some have concluded, therefore, that Jesus' behaviour was in open defiance of the law.[82] However, the law does not forbid eating with those who do not themselves observe the laws of cleanliness and tithing, even though this was a reasonable way of expanding it,[83] and as far as we know the Pharisaic programme was not widely accepted as authoritative either before 70 C.E. or immediately after it.

It is not stated, of course, whether Jesus kept the laws on cleanliness and tithing, though it is implied that he did not. The most we can conclude is that prior to 70 C.E. such actions would have been seen as a challenge to the Pharisaic interpretation of the law rather than the law itself. If by Luke's day the Pharisaic campaign had met with greater success, Jesus' action could have been seen as a challenge to the Jewish legal system as he knew it, in which rabbinic interpretation of the law was increasingly accorded the same authority as Torah. More than this we cannot say.

A similar issue arises in Lk. 11:37–41 in a discussion between Jesus and his Pharisaic host over the question of ceremonial cleanliness. Jesus' failure to wash before eating occasions surprise, to which he responds with the obscure and somewhat ungracious words (verses 39–41): 'You Pharisees clean the outside of the cup and plate, but inside you are full of rapacity and wickedness. Fools, did not he who made the outside also make the inside? Rather, give alms from that which is within, and behold everything is clean to you.' With the addition of ὑμῶν (verse 39 cf. Matt. 23:25) Luke indicates that he understands the words as an extended analogy between utensils and men. The maker (verse 40) may refer to God or man and 'that which is within' (verse 41) to the contents of the cups and dishes or men's possessions in general. The peculiarly Lucan allusion to almsgiving expresses a theme to which he constantly returns. As so often when challenged, Jesus replies obliquely; but there is no mistaking the rejection of the Pharisaic position, even though this may be subsidiary to the theme of almsgiving. How this was viewed by Luke and his readers again depends on how precise their knowledge of Judaism was and how successfully the Pharisaic–rabbinic programme had been extended. The concluding statement – 'and behold everything is clean to you' – could be taken to imply a rejection of the laws of cleanliness in favour of works of compassion. The effect on the Pharisaic–rabbinic position, indeed on the very distinction between clean and unclean, would be drastic (cf. Mk 7:15). However no such conclusions are drawn and the saying is juxtaposed to one which suggests a quite different assessment of Pharisaic scrupulosity (verse 42). From one curious juxtaposition we now turn to another.

C. Luke 16:16–18

The passage we are about to consider is the only notable discussion of the status of the law in Luke's Gospel:

> The law and the prophets were until John; since then the good news of the kingdom of God is preached, and everyone enters it violently. But it is easier for heaven and earth to pass away than for one dot of the law to become void. Everyone who divorces his wife and marries another commits adultery, and he who marries a woman divorced from her husband commits adultery.

In terms of both content and context these words must surely be as obscure as anything in the synoptic tradition. One of the problems has been illustrated in the preceding discussion, where each verse has deliberately been used as evidence for a different attitude towards the law. The parallels in Matthew are found separately and in different contexts. Lk. 16:17 is related to Matt. 5:18 and Lk. 16:18 to Matt. 5:32f, while Lk. 16:16 appears in a different form in Matt. 11:12–13. Since they fit uneasily into their present context, having at best a loose connection with Lk. 16:29, 31, and since in comparison with Matthew Luke clearly provides the *connexio difficilior*, both the juxtaposition of the three sayings and their location in this context are thought to be pre-Lucan.[84] This may well be so, although the riddle is scarcely solved by placing it at an earlier stage of redaction.

Lk. 16:16 has been much discussed by those concerned with the eschatology of Jesus or the position of John the Baptist in Luke's scheme of salvation-history. Neither of these is of immediate concern to us and many complex exegetical disputes can be ignored. Thus whether John stands within or beyond the era designated as the 'law and the prophets' ($\mu\acute{\epsilon}\chi\rho\iota$ and $\dot{\alpha}\pi\grave{o}$ $\tau\acute{o}\tau\epsilon$ are ambiguous), and whether the ambiguous $\beta\iota\acute{\alpha}\zeta\epsilon\tau\alpha\iota$ is used in a good or a bad sense and to whom it refers[85] are issues which do not significantly affect the question of the law. For our purposes the crucial issue is the relationship between the law and the prophets (16*a*) and the preaching of the kingdom (16*b*). If we isolate verse 16 from its context, verse 16*b* suggests some sort of limitation of the era of the law and the prophets. The announcement of the kingdom could imply the demise of the former era and must at least imply that a significant new element has been added. The ambiguity can only be resolved by the context and that, as we shall see, offers little help. The meaning of the phrase 'the law and the prophets' is also unclear. It occurs frequently in Luke (Lk. 16:16; 24:27, 44; Ac. 13:15; 24:14; 28:23) and Matthew (Matt. 5:17; 7:12; 11:13; 22:40) but rarely elsewhere in the New Testament (Rom. 3:21; Jn 1:45). Berger suggests that in Lk. 16:16/Matt. 11:13, and possibly in the other Matthean passages too, it refers to the will of God as expressed in the Old Testament. It rests, he argues, on an Old Testament and Jewish tradition which sees the prophets as interpreters of the law and Moses as one of the prophets. Both are concerned with the same thing – declaring the will of God (II Kings 17:13; Dan. 9:5–6; IV Ezr. 7:129f; Test. Lev. 16:2; Jos. *Ant.* IX.281, etc.). Since 'preaching the kingdom' in Luke means primarily a call to repentance, the function of the law and the prophets is understood similarly. Both call men to repentance, the main difference being that 'all' (πᾶς verse 16*b*) are invited into the kingdom.[86] This may be correct, but Berger can provide no evidence outside the synoptics for the use of the phrase 'the law and the prophets' in this way and, as he himself notes, all the other occurrences in Luke–Acts concern the predictive or prophetic function of the Old Testament, especially in christological contexts. Here the law and the prophets are understood as the promise of which Jesus' career is the fulfilment, and it may well be that in Lk. 16:16 Luke understood the phrase in the same way (cf. Matthew's addition of ἐπροφήτευσαν in 11:13) even if originally it meant something different. Either interpretation provides a contrast between the law and the prophets and the kingdom: in Berger's view the one revelation of the will of God has been supplemented by another doing the same thing but in a universal context; in the other view the law and the prophets signify the era of promise of which the message of the kingdom is the fulfilment. The preaching of the kingdom, understood broadly as in Acts as the Christian gospel,[87] fulfils the promises of God in the Old Testament.

The next verse picks up the theme of law but does not mention the prophets. Matthew's version (5:18) – which opens with 'Truly, I say to you', adds a reference to 'one iota', and concludes with the ambiguous words 'until all things come to pass' – is usually considered to be secondary to Luke's briefer form of the saying.[88] The phrase τοῦ νόμου μίαν κεραίαν indicates that the whole of the law, in all its details, is meant and not just its 'moral demands'[89] or its 'ideal contents'.[90] It would seem therefore to be a different use of νόμος from that in verse 16*a*. The statement that 'it is easier (εὐκοπώτερον) for heaven and earth to pass away . . . ', in conjunction with μία κεραία, is commonly understood as an expression of the absolute and eternal value of the law.[91] In contrast to

Matthew who, it is claimed, sets a *terminus ad quem* by his addition of ἕως ἄν πάντα γένηται, Luke does not reckon seriously with the passing away of heaven and earth or of the law. It may be, however, that it expresses the extreme difficulty, rather than the impossibility, of altering the law. The word εὐκοπώτερον, which does not occur in Matt. 5:18, is used in a formally identical saying in Lk. 18:25 (Mk 10:25; Matt. 19:24): 'It is easier (εὐκοπώτερον) for a camel to go through the eye of a needle than for a rich man to enter the kingdom of God.' If this analogy is taken literally then clearly it is impossible for the rich to enter the kingdom – for it certainly is impossible for a camel to go through the eye of a needle. The context suggests, however, that we are dealing with deliberate hyperbole, since the parallel saying which introduces the pericope speaks of the difficulty rather than the impossibility of the rich entering the kingdom (verse 24) and the concluding observation notes that what men cannot achieve God can (verse 27). Perhaps by way of analogy Lk. 16:17 should be read in the same way, for the passing of heaven and earth is no less likely than a camel negotiating the eye of a needle. Of course, the meaning of Lk. 18:25 is suggested by its context and Lk. 16:17 is not provided with an equally helpful setting. But the context has led some, quite apart from any analogy with Lk. 18:25, to suppose that Lk. 16:17 is a hyperbole which speaks of the extreme difficulty rather than the impossibility of voiding the law.[92]

This leads us naturally to Lk. 16:18, the only occasion on which the topic of remarriage and divorce is broached in Luke's Gospel. In exhaustive discussions of the relationship of this saying to the discussion in Mk 10:2–12/Matt. 19:1–9 and the sayings in Matt. 5:32f no consensus has been reached, but the distinctiveness of Luke's version remains clear whether this verse, Matt. 5:32, or some combination of the two, is thought to be the earliest form of the saying.[93] The condemnation of remarriage of divorcees, which at the same time implies a condemnation of divorce as such, as far as we can tell runs counter to both current Jewish practice and the Mosaic law which, though not commanding divorce, assume its legality by setting out appropriate procedures. In contrast to Mark and Matthew there is in Luke no reference to an ordinance of creation whereby one part of the Mosaic writings is used to explain another. The absence of this line of argument can be understood in at least two ways. On the one hand, since the use of one passage of scripture to expose the real intention of another – a common enough procedure in rabbinic reasoning – softens the ostensible rejection of a Mosaic ordinance, its absence from Luke makes his version a starker and bolder challenge to the Mosaic law. On the other hand, it might be noted that Luke thereby avoids a certain denigration of the law implied by the Markan notion that some Mosaic ordinances were based solely on a concession to human sinfulness.

It might be argued that Lk. 16:18 is less an abrogation and more an intensification of the law and as such akin to the scribal 'building a hedge around the law'. Moreover if, as seems probable, the Qumran community took an equally stringent view of divorce (CD 4:20–5:12),[94] this could be taken to show that increasing the demands of the law in precisely this fashion could be seen as an expression of total commitment to the law rather than as a challenge to its authority. The problem with the Qumran analogy, however, is that it rests upon the view which a sectarian minority had of themselves, and this might have been very different from the view which other Jews had of them. Moreover, although the Qumran evidence may shed light on the conversations about divorce among Jesus and his contemporaries, by the time Luke wrote the Qumran centre had been destroyed and the remnants of the community scattered. There is no evidence that their teaching on divorce had the slightest influence on the forms of Judaism likely to have been known to Luke and his readers. The parallel with the scribal procedure of 'building a hedge around the law' is also imprecise. The purpose of this procedure, with respect to the issue at hand, can be expressed approximately as follows: 'To avoid divorcing for the wrong reasons, do not divorce at all.' This line of reasoning is not evident in Luke any more than it is in the lengthier discussion in Mk. 10:2f. It is in fact difficult to find a rabbinic parallel in which building a hedge around the law intensifies its demands in such a way that it contradicts the Mosaic ruling which is being protected. Disputes over the minimum and maximum application of the law, as between the schools of Hillel and Shammai, were common enough; but the point was rarely, if ever, to dispute the authority of the Torah as such. The point of halakic rulings was, by and large, to define the extent to which the rules of the Torah applied. As the rabbinic discussion of divorce shows, the usual procedure was not to sweep aside the Mosaic ordinance in favour of some more stringent ruling but to define the precise extent of its application. There are exceptions, when halakic rulings circumscribe or even prevent the application of Torah in its plain sense. The Mishnah records (Shebiith 10.3–4) that Hillel devised a scheme which circumvented the rule about sabbatical release of debts (Dt. 15:1f) to encourage lending, but it was also justified by the desire to avoid fraud and oppression as defined in Dt. 15:9. Again, while Torah was thought to require that the donation of the Temple tax or the presentation of a bill of divorce had to be done willingly (Lev. 1:3), a man could be coerced until he said, 'I am willing' (Arak. 5:6). These and similar examples are marked by a degree of legal fiction, a tendency to relax rather than intensify the demands of the law, and a conviction that the true intention of scripture was being fulfilled. Insofar as they do provide a parallel to the Gospel teaching on divorce it is to the type of discussion recorded in Mk 10 rather than to the isolated assertion of Lk. 16. It seems fair to conclude that any Christian author or reader after 70 C.E., who knew the ruling of Moses in Deuteronomy and current Jewish custom, would most naturally have understood Lk. 16:18 as a challenge to the authority of the one and the practice of the other.

We are now in a position to consider some of the attempts to understand the meaning of these three verses in their Lucan context. Conzelmann, as we have seen, suggests that verse 16 must be interpreted by verse 17. Since the latter asserts the lasting value of the law, the former cannot mean the opposite. While originally verse 16 may have meant that the law and the prophets had been superseded by the kingdom, for Luke it meant that in the new era they coexisted: 'In other words, the epochs are separate, but there is no break between them, for the elements of the former one persist into the next.'[95] Conzelmann is aware that the law and the prophets together form the basis both of the call to repentance and of the proof from prophecy, but thinks the former sense is intended in verses 16–17. The law, as a call to repentance, is confirmed, but it is tied to a particular phase of the Church; after the apostolic decree it is no longer in force.

This analysis is neither clear nor convincing. To some degree Conzelmann's interpretation illustrates the confusion already present in the Lucan writings and it is clear that he has some difficulty finding a coherent sense for verses 16–17. He does so in part by ignoring verse 18 altogether and in part by understanding law as the basis for a call to repentance, which is not the most natural meaning of νόμος in verse 17. Introducing the apostolic decree adds to the confusion, for if we allow that it marks the end of legal obligations for the Church — a view which is questionable for Gentile, let alone Jewish, Christians — it would seem that it is the legal obligations implied by verse 17, rather than the law as a call to repentance, which are abandoned. It is at any rate wholly arbitrary to introduce the apostolic decree as the terminus for verse 17 when that verse has just been used to interpret verse 16 to mean that the law has abiding validity.

Berger concurs with Conzelmann in some respects.[96] The 'law and the prophets' in verse 16*a* is not a reference to the Old Testament as scripture or a collection of proof texts but as the revelation of the will of God. The same function is performed by the preaching of the kingdom, except that 'all' are invited. The law is not done away with (verse 17) for the law, the prophets and Christian preaching all perform the same task — announcing the will of God and calling for repentance. Lk. 16:29, 31 return to this theme, verse 29 linking up with verses 16–18 and verse 31 looking forward to the post-resurrection mission to the Jews. Christian preaching of the resurrection, like the call of Moses and the prophets, meets with the same disbelief. Berger recognizes the shift in the use of νόμος between verse 16 and verse 17, but suggests that although νόμος in verse 17 clearly refers to the commands of the law, the law is understood as an expression of the will of God in a way not wholly dissimilar to verse 16. This is possible, although it depends on interpreting 'the law and the prophets' in verse 16 differently from other uses of the same phrase in Luke–Acts. The connection with 16:29, 31 is feasible, but may be fortuitous, and 18:18 cannot readily be linked in the same way. Berger, like Conzelmann, offers no solution to the link between verses 16–17 and verse 18, except to say that verse 18 is a particular example of the νόμος referred to in verse 17!

Daube suggests that three pieces of Jewish evidence might throw some light on these verses.[97] He draws first on Philo (*Vit. Mos.* II.3.14f), who associated the permanence of the Torah and its universal attractiveness, a connection of ideas which Luke has in reverse order in verses 16–17. He then refers to a rabbinic tradition that the returning Elijah would be entitled to alter the law, suggesting that if in the original context, as in Matthew (11:12–13), John was associated with Elijah, this may have provoked an immediate clarification that the law would not be changed. Finally, he recalls the story of the personified Deuteronomy in heaven accusing Solomon of annulling the law by reading Dt. 17:17 not as 'he shall not multiply wives to himself' but as 'to a multitude of wives for himself'. God's comforting reply was that 'Solomon and a thousand like him will perish, but a word of yours will not perish' (p. Sanh. 20*c*; Ex. Rabba on 6:2). Since the Zadokite fragments (7.1f) use Dt. 17:17 to prohibit polygamy and divorce, the notion that the neglect of this precept implied the neglect of the whole law may be earlier than the rabbinic tradition just quoted. It seems doubtful, however, that Daube's evidence sheds any light on the Lucan form of these sayings. It is disparate, coming from different times and places; the Philonic notion does not parallel the Lucan contrast between law and kingdom; the tradition about Elijah plays only a minor role in rabbinic thinking; and the association of Dt. 17:17 with a prohibition of divorce is not found in rabbinic tradition. It is even doubtful that the Qumran prohibition sheds light on Luke's understanding of these words, although it may be of more use if they are taken to be the words of the historical Jesus.

Derrett's proposal for understanding the connection between verses

16—18 and their context is equally improbable.[98] He understands 16:1—8 as a critique of the rabbinic laws of usury which, by allowing certain types of usury, had undermined the absolute prohibition in the law. The 'all' who rush to enter the kingdom are Gentiles and it is immediately pointed out that this does not substantially affect the status of the law or God's relationship with Israel (verse 17). The following verse (verse 18) recalls the theme of 16:1—8 by giving a parallel case to usury in which Jesus condemns the way in which a Mosaic concession had been expanded into a norm justifying all divorce. That 'all' in verse 16 includes Gentiles is possible but improbable, but there is nothing to suggest that it excludes Jews. The interpretation of verse 18 is effected by importing a distinction made in Mk 10:2f but not in Luke and, as Derrett himself is aware, his explanation provides no convincing reason for the location of verse 16 in its present position.

Schürmann approaches the problem obliquely in the course of his discussion of the provenance of Matt. 5:19.[99] He concludes that it stood in Q between Lk. 16:17 and Lk. 16:18 and he reconstructs the source as follows: Lk. 16:14—17, Matt. 5:19, and Lk. 16:18. The missing verse (Matt. 5:19) originally expressed the practical consequences of the formal statement in Lk. 16:17 whose unusually sharp thesis, he thinks, needed explanation or qualification. Lk. 16:14—18 as it stands is a torso and must originally have been embedded in a more comprehensive discussion of the law — a theme which Schürmann thinks was of no great interest to Luke. He explains Luke's omission of Matt. 5:19 and retention of Lk. 16:14—18 as follows: Lk. 16:14—15 serve as the conclusion to 15:1—16:13; 16:18 is retained because divorce was a live issue in Gentile communities; 16:16 introduces 16:18; and 16:17, where νόμος means the ethical demands of God rather than the Torah as a whole, is a general statement of which verse 18 is a particular example. The extreme nomistic claims of Matt. 5:19 are passed over as inappropriate to the context and irrelevant to Luke's readers. The whole of Lk. 16:16—18 is thus understood in an antinomistic fashion: the law and the prophets have been fulfilled and superseded by the kingdom (verse 16); but the law, understood solely as the ethical demands of God, remains in force (verse 17) — as Jesus' ruling on divorce reveals (verse 18).

Despite his exhaustively detailed discussion, Schürmann fails to provide any convincing evidence that Matt. 5:19 stood in that version of Q from which Luke took 16:14—18 (assuming for the moment the two-document hypothesis). Even if we grant him that, however, the reasons he proposes for Luke's omission of the saying are scarcely convincing. There is no evidence that Luke understood νόμος in verse 17 or elsewhere to mean solely the ethical commands of God. They are of course included in, but by no means exhaust, the meaning of νόμος in Luke—Acts. Again, even if Schürmann was right in this assumption we might still wonder why, if Luke could understand Lk. 16:17 in this way, he could not have understood Matt. 5:19 similarly and included it. For if 'one dot of the law' (Lk. 16:17) could be understood in this way why not 'one of the least of these commands' (Matt. 5:19) too? We might also note in passing that some believe Matt. 5:19 softens the impact of 5:18 (= Lk. 16:17), insofar as it recognizes that those who do relax the commands have a place in the kingdom even if it is the lowest,[100] which would mean that Luke contains the more, rather than the less, nomistic of the two sayings.

Banks, whose main interest is in the original meaning of Lk. 16:16—18 pars., makes passing reference to the use Matthew and Luke make of them.[101] Despite their differences, he notes, both writers emphasize that a decisive change is signalled by the arrival of the kingdom (Lk. 16:16; Matt. 11:12—13) but neither concludes that the law has been abrogated (Lk. 16:17; Matt. 5:18). The law survives, however, in terms not of its own demands but of those of the kingdom; it is valid only insofar as it is transformed and fulfilled in the teaching of Jesus. Lk. 16:17 is a rhetorical assertion of how difficult it is for the law to perish and not a claim for its eternal validity, and Banks would presumably understand verse 18 as an example of the claims of the kingdom superseding those of the law.[102] He thinks that Lk. 16:16—18 is an anomaly in Luke's Gospel, since nowhere else do we find any interest in the theme of law *per se*, and the inclusion of verses 17—18 shows Luke's faithfulness to tradition rather than his concern for the law. Together with some useful observations there is, however, an underlying inconsistency in Banks' analysis. Thus Lk. 16:17 is on some occasions used to show that the law has not been abrogated and on other occasions interpreted to mean that the law can, under some circumstances, be altered. To assert that the law remains valid only insofar as it is transformed by and fulfilled in the teaching of Jesus leads irresistibly to the conclusion that it has been set aside.

If it does nothing else, this review of recent attempts to find a coherent thread running through Lk. 16:16—18 shows that it is no mean task. The problem is most clearly exposed by considering the ways in which these verses might have been understood. On the one hand, they might have been interpreted as an affirmation of the law. Lk. 16:16 is a statement of fact: until John the law and the prophets performed their task — understood to be prophetic, predictive or more generally as an expression of the will of God; since then the Christian message has been preached and either opposed or energetically welcomed (depending on the meaning of βιάζεται). But this does not mean that the law has been superseded, for it will not pass away (verse 17); its demands are still valid and have been intensified and extended in the teaching of Jesus (verse 18).[103] For such an interpretation verse 17 is crucial and is used to interpret the verses on either side of it. In particular, Jesus' teaching on remarriage and divorce is seen as a positive extension rather than an abrogation of the law, and this has the advantage of underlining 16:29, 31 which appear to affirm the law too.

The main stumbling block to such a view is the final verse which, as we have seen, would most likely have been seen by Luke and his readers as a challenge to a Mosaic ordinance as well as to current Jewish thinking. If this is taken as the starting point a quite different interpretation is required. Lk. 16:16 would then be seen to introduce a contrast between two eras — in which the era of the law and the prophets, however understood, is superseded or fulfilled by the era of the kingdom — and Lk. 16:17 would be seen as an assertion of the difficulty rather than the impossibility of changing the law. The analogy with the passing away of heaven and earth emphasizes that annulment of the law can occur with only the most extraordinary intervention — either the coming of the kingdom (verse 16), the teaching of Jesus (verse 18), or both.

The ambiguity of Lk. 16:16—18 epitomizes the ambiguity of Luke's Gospel as a whole, in which the law is both upheld and challenged, so that we cannot resolve the problem of these verses by evidence from elsewhere in the Gospel. Yet this may suggest another alternative for understanding Lk. 16:16—18, namely that Luke did not intend to offer a consistent view of the law here or elsewhere. The connection between them, whether we put it down to Luke or a predecessor, may be no more profound than that they all deal, in different ways, with the law. Lk. 16:16 may express the theme of promise and fulfilment so prominent elsewhere in Luke—Acts. Lk. 16:17 may have been attached solely because of the link word νόμος, though using it in a different sense and dealing with the prescriptive rather than the predictive function of the law, and Lk. 16:18 because it expresses judgement on a legal matter, even though it does not use the word νόμος. In other words we may have here three discrete sayings linked by a common theme but not by a consistent approach to it.

D. Lucan omissions?

The absence from Luke of two significant Markan passages dealing with the law (Mk 7:1—21; 10:2—12) calls for some comment since, whatever view we take of synoptic relationships, it has an effect on the overall presentation of this theme as compared with Matthew and Mark. We shall again assume the two-document hypothesis for the sake of argument. The first passage in Mark traverses several themes: unclean hands (verses 1–8), the corban oath (verses 9–13), and inner/outer purity (verses 14–21). With respect to the law two major conclusions emerge. First, there is an explicit rejection of Pharisaic tradition (wrongly ascribed to all Jews in verse 3) which, while purporting to be an interpretation of the law, is judged to have undermined the commands of God. The criticism is sharp and uncompromising and the examples used are considered symptomatic of a widespread disease (verse 13). Second, a profound and radical criticism of the law itself is expressed in verses 14f by the declaration that, since nothing from outside can defile a man, all foods are clean (verse 19). Not only are the food laws of Leviticus implicitly rejected but the distinction between clean and unclean, widespread in the ancient world, is also dramatically overturned.

The absence of this material cannot be discussed without reference to the problem of the so-called 'great omission' of Mk 6:45–8:27 from Luke. Broadly speaking there are two types of explanation: that the omission is accidental since Luke did not know this section of Mark, or that it is deliberate because he did not approve of it. The former view, given its classic expression by Streeter,[104] is by far the most persuasive if only because it is almost impossible to construct a convincing case for the latter. On the one hand, since no single explanation is sufficient to explain the omission of all the material, several explanations must be combined – and the more they multiply the less they convince. On the other hand, it is hard to find a plausible explanation for the omission of such a large block of *continuous* material. The notion of deliberate omission would be initially more plausible if the pericopes had been scattered throughout Mark but, as things stand, accidental omission is the simplest and neatest explanation. Nevertheless there has been no shortage of attempts to clarify Luke's intention. The avoidance of doublets might explain the omission of the feeding (Mk 8:1–10), but not much else. The suggestion[105] that it was the geographical framework rather than the contents to which Luke objected is open to doubt, for even if Luke was trying to confine Jesus' activity to a particular area, he could have edited the framework and kept the contents as he does elsewhere. The most detailed recent attempt to defend the theory of deliberate omission is that of Schürmann.[106] Eschewing a single explanation, he combines three: the avoidance of doublets; the redactional interests of the author; and the omission of material no longer of significance to Luke's communities. The evidence for the last two, however, is not forthcoming. The problem of unclean hands, for example, is introduced in the third Gospel and given a specifically Lucan twist (Lk. 11:37f). Why could he not have done the same with Mk 7:1f? Moreover, the question of unclean foods arises in Ac. 10–11 and was presumably therefore of some interest to Luke and his readers. Indeed, Hübner argues that it is precisely because the issue is taken up in Ac. 10–11 that it is omitted from the Gospel, where it would have undermined Luke's careful scheme of salvation-history.[107] The omission of Mk 7:24f is also difficult to explain since it would have been an ideal expression of Luke's interest in the Gentile mission. Overall, Schürmann's argument is a good illustration of how difficult it is to explain adequately the omission of each pericope and at the same time convince us that it is mere coincidence that they are linked into a continuous narrative by Mark.

In terms of the two-document hypothesis the most likely explanation for the absence of Mk 7:1–23 is, therefore, a simple one: it was not in Luke's version of Mark. He did not omit it because it was too radical, since elsewhere he includes criticism of both Pharisaic tradition and the law itself; nor is he concerned to preserve a careful scheme of salvation-history in which Jesus and the early Church are strictly law-abiding up to the beginning of the Gentile mission. It was not in Luke because it was not in his source.

The same argument does not apply to Mk 10:2–12, unless one resorts to the hypothesis of an *Ur-Markus* to which this pericope did not belong. An adequate explanation is in fact hard to come by. It cannot be that Luke objected to Jesus' teaching on divorce since he includes it in slightly different form in Lk. 16:18. The conflict with the teaching of Moses is not explicit in Luke's version, but to any reader for whom this was a problem the challenge to Dt. 24:1f and current Jewish thinking would have been immediately obvious. Omitting the preliminary discussion does little to minimize this effect and may even enhance it. If it is thought that Luke was uneasy with the polarization of the Mosaic ordinance and God's plan at creation, where one part of the law is used to undermine another, it should be remembered that he uses a similar argument in Lk. 6:1–5 and that the allusion to Gen. 2:24 arguably reduces the offensiveness of Jesus' teaching whereas Lk. 16:18 gives it starker expression. Perhaps the explanation is simpler, namely that Luke and his readers were interested only in the teaching of Jesus on remarriage and divorce – an issue of some consequence in all Christian communities – but not in the question of its relationship to the law or Jewish thinking. One might naturally conclude from this that Luke was writing primarily for Gentile Christians for whom the law, or at least those aspects of it over which Jesus and his contemporaries disputed, was not a major concern. Certainly, whatever view we take of synoptic relationships, the effect of the absence of these two passages is to deprive Luke's Gospel of almost all theoretical discussion about the law. The same tendency is evident in Lk. 10:25f and the overall impression, as compared with Matthew and Mark, is that theoretical discussion of the status and interpretation of the law, or the ranking of specific commandments within it, was of little interest to Luke and those for whom he wrote.

E. Conclusions

As we noted earlier, the theme of law in Luke's Gospel has not been the subject of much scholarly discussion. Conzelmann has a few things to say and his view is developed briefly by Hübner. Banks who, like Hübner, is concerned with Jesus' teaching, also has some concluding remarks on Luke's presentation. The most recent essay devoted entirely to the topic, by Jervell, covers the Gospel and Acts but takes most of its evidence from the latter. Our remaining task is to sketch these views and assess them against the conclusions reached so far.

Conzelmann has little to say on the law as a theme in Luke's Gospel and his understanding of it is controlled almost exclusively by Lk. 16:16–17.[108] For Luke the law is not simply command nor the prophets simply prophecy. Law and prophets go hand in hand, for both prophesy and both command. Together they form the basis of both the call to repentance and the scheme of proof from prophecy. The prophetic aspect of the law is expressed most obviously in Lk. 24:27, 44 and is illustrated in Lk. 1–2. The juxtaposition of Lk. 16:16 and 16:17 reveals that while there is a distinction between the epoch of law and that of the kingdom, the elements of the former persist into the latter. The law and the prophets, understood as a call to repentance, co-exist with the message of the kingdom, and the law is thus carefully slotted into Luke's conception of salvation-history. The early Church and Paul keep the law without exception. The turning point comes at the apostolic council (Ac. 15) when an ecclesiastical decree, distinguishing between two phases of the Church's existence, frees Christians from the law. Hübner[109] utilizes this schematic outline to understand Luke's presentation of Jesus and the law – a topic which, on the whole, Conzelmann neglects. Luke, he thinks, denies any abrogation of the law by Jesus and this explains his juxtaposition of 16:16 and 16:17 and his omission of Mk 10:2f. He takes over material which contradicts his view but minimizes it either by failing to signal the abrogation of the law or by juxtaposing it with corrective material. Lk. 16:16 is to be interpreted, with Conzelmann, to mean that in the new epoch the law and the prophets and the message of the kingdom co-exist. Luke does this not because he was a nomist but because he is tied to a scheme of salvation-history in which the time for abrogation of the law falls in the era of the Church. He thus omits Mk 7:1–23 but introduces the same issue in Ac. 10–11. Both the career and the teaching of Jesus are understood by the scheme of promise and fulfilment. He is thus supported by the authority of the law and the prophets, but does not stand authoritatively over them. Fulfilment of the law, for Luke, does not mean modification of it.

Jervell, for quite different reasons, comes to the same conclusion – that Luke presents Jesus as living wholly in conformity with the law. Indeed, in view of the refutation of the charges against Stephen in Ac. 6:11f and the depiction of Jewish-Christians as zealots for the law in Ac. 21:21, Luke was bound to present Jesus as upholding the law. Thus there is no discussion in Luke about greater and lesser commands (Mk 12:28f), Mk 10:2–9 is omitted and, in the absence of Mk 7:1–23, there is no rejection of the oral law as the mere customs of men. When his interest in almsgiving intrudes into the discussion of ritual cleanliness it does not result in criticism of the law or scribal tradition. In the sabbath conflicts there is no conflict with the law, since the Jewish leaders are unable to raise objections either to his actions or to his rationale for them. Jervell's conclusion is that 'Luke has the most conservative outlook within the New Testament, because of his concern for the law as Israel's law, the sign of God's people.'[110]

Characteristic of the views just outlined is the attempt to find a consistent approach to the law in the Gospel and Acts. This is understandable and legitimate as long as it is not based on an *a priori* assumption that a coherent view is necessarily present. That Luke has a consistent view throughout his two volumes must be proven rather than assumed, and there is always the danger that the more consistent view of Acts will be imposed on the Gospel. Banks,[111] on the other hand, deals solely with the evidence in the Gospel and concludes that the issue of the law held no specific interest for Luke. He never develops a theological answer to the problem and the only overt discussion of it (Lk. 16:16–18) is in a context where it is subordinate to the motif of behaviour appropriate to the kingdom. He omits (Mk 7:1–23; 10:2–12) or alters (Lk. 10:25f) discussions over the nature of the law, and the sabbath disputes are concerned with christological rather than legal matters. Jesus' implicit stance, however, is not conservative, as is seen most clearly in the sabbath stories. Luke's view is dominated by christology – Jesus' preaching, teaching and healing ministry which calls men to salvation – and, though not explicitly, it is this which for Luke supersedes the law. The saving ministry of Jesus is seen as the fulfilment of all that was promised to Israel (Lk. 4:16f; 24:44f)

– and this applies to the legal material as well. He remarks in passing that the Gospel evidence is not easily brought into line with the ostensibly more conservative stance of Acts.

Our discussion has elicited a variety of emphases from Luke's Gospel which can be summarized as follows:

(1) The law is occasionally given a prophetic function, explicitly and programmatically in Lk. 24:27, 44 and perhaps allusively in Lk. 16:16; 9:29, 33. It is seen as one component of the promises to Israel – together with the prophets and, in one case, the Psalms (24:44) – which find their fulfilment in the person and work of Jesus. This theme is less prominent in the Gospel than in Acts but it is nevertheless a significant component in his conception of the law. It exists side by side, but not integrated, with the other concepts of the law.

(2) The commands of the law are affirmed (Lk. 10:25f; 16:17; 16:29, 31; 18:18f cf. 11:42), especially the two love commands (10:25f; 11:42). What this signifies in practice is illustrated in the birth narratives and later in the ministry of Jesus (Lk. 1–2; 4:16, 40; 5:14, 39; 17:14 cf. 22:56). Luke seems to emphasize two related themes: first, that the law is an adequate guide for the pious and godly whose goal is entry into the kingdom; and second, that doing the law rather than discussing it is of paramount importance. The reverse of this lies in the condemnation of those who abuse and disobey the commands of God (Lk. 7:27f, 36f; 11:37– 12:3; 15:2f; 16:14–15; 18:9–14; 19:39, 45f; 20:1–26, 45–7). The attack is not on the law itself but on men's failure to keep it. The demands of the law are an accurate expression of the will of God and a reliable guide to practical piety.

(3) The status of the law and some specific commands within it are undermined by the teaching of Jesus which ignores (Lk. 6:12f), supplements (Lk. 18:18f cf. 16:16), or seriously calls it into question (Lk. 6:1–11; 13:10–17; 14:1–6; 11:41; 16:18 cf. 5:17f, 33f; 9:60). This subversion of the law is rarely explicit, the clearest examples being the sabbath controversies and the divorce saying, and potentially radical sayings are often insulated by their immediate surroundings (11:41; 16:18). Luke rarely signals conflict with the law but neither does he make much effort to cover it up. In some cases he seems more concerned with the christological than with the legal implications of specific incidents.

(4) The ambiguity of Luke's presentation is most pointed in those passages where potentially contradictory sayings are closely juxtaposed (11:41–2; 16:16–18). He makes no obvious attempt to resolve the ambiguity. He does not, for example, call on the distinction between oral

and written law, nor does he relish debates over light and weighty commands or indeed over the law in general.

It is virtually impossible to construct a consistent pattern from this evidence, even if we agree that Luke has not attempted this himself. He presents Jesus as sometimes opposed to and sometimes in league with the law. He does not stand under the law as Hübner and Jervell suppose, nor essentially above it as Banks suggests. For a reader of Luke's Gospel either conclusion is defensible – an ambiguity which is most pointed in 16:16–18. Glancing momentarily into Acts, it is noteworthy that the muted theological critique of the law as a means of salvation (Ac. 13:39; 15:10–11) is nowhere suggested in the Gospel. If anything, the opposite is maintained (Lk. 10:25f). And if the denial of the accusation against Stephen (Ac. 6:11f) refers not merely to what Stephen said or to what Jesus might do but also to what Jesus had done, a reader of the Gospel might conclude from some of the material that the charge was indeed justified!

The variety of Lucan material on the law and the absence of any clear signs of reflection on it, in marked contrast to Matthew and Mark, suggest that the question of Jesus' attitude towards the law was not a problem for Luke and his readers, at least at the time he composed the Gospel. For this reason he can use inconsistent material to emphasize different themes in connection with the law – prophetic, practical or christological – without feeling obliged to knit them into a whole. It was not necessary for him either to defend Jesus against a charge of antinomianism or to present a christology which affirmed or redefined the issue. And thus the answer to our own question in the sub-heading 'Challenging the law?' is that the challenge is at most implicit, and even then it is evidence more for Luke's indifference towards the problem than for anything else.

On the basis of our discussion so far we can be fairly sure that Luke stands at a considerable distance from the concerns of rabbinic Judaism as it developed after 70 C.E. This is clear not only from the frequent castigation of the scribes and Pharisees but also in the disputes over specific issues, such as sabbath observance and ritual cleanliness, and in the teaching on divorce. One cannot simply conclude from this that Luke was opposed to the Pharisees and rabbis as such (cf. 11:42). Some of their teaching is challenged, but it is their failure to live up to their own ideals which is Luke's greater concern. On the other hand, some of the material which broaches the topic of law, especially those passages which emphasize obedience to its central demands, recalls similar attitudes among hellenistic-Jewish writers.[112]

It is possible that among Luke's readers there were Jewish-Christians whose roots were in a diaspora Judaism which had already developed a different approach from rabbinic circles to the law and whose faith in Jesus had led to further revision of their attitude towards legal matters. Presumably they would have been different from the Jewish-Christians for whom Matthew wrote and for whom Jesus' attitude towards the law was a problem — but there is nothing inherently improbable in this. It is my hunch, however, that the simplest explanation is that Luke wrote mainly, if not solely, for Gentile Christians for whom those aspects of the law discussed in the Gospel were not a problem. If this was so, then we might go on to say that, with a few exceptions, the impression conveyed to such readers would have been largely positive. That is, the criticism of the law is generally implicit and has to be read between the lines, whereas the affirmation of the law is generally explicit. If they had no incentive to read between the lines, they would have received a vague but positive impression from which they might have concluded that the law remained a valid guide for Jews and Jewish-Christians, since it gave an accurate account both of the promises of God fulfilled in Jesus and of the behaviour God requires of men. Of course, for Luke and his readers legal piety would need to be informed by Christian belief, but it need not thereby be annulled; and, naturally, the problem of its relevance for Gentiles did not arise at this stage of the narrative.

3 THE LAW IN ACTS

A. Law and salvation

On two occasions we are provided with casual, muted echoes of the intense debate surrounding the law in the Pauline era. The essential issue for Luke, as for Paul, was the relationship between keeping the law and receiving salvation. In Ac. 13:38–9 the following words are placed on the lips of Paul: 'Let it be known to you therefore brethren that through this man forgiveness of sins is proclaimed to you, and by him everyone that believes is freed (δικαιωθῆναι) from everything from which you could not be freed by the law of Moses.' It has long been recognized that while these words echo Pauline language they do not express Pauline thought with any precision. The gist seems clear enough: there are things which the law of Moses cannot provide but which the gospel of Christ can. It is difficult to be more precise about the contrast, although in view of the virtual equivalence of 'forgiveness of sins' and 'justification/exoneration' – which has a Lucan rather than a Pauline ring to it (cf. Lk. 1:77; 14:37) – the contrast is probably to be found in this connection. That is, if ὧν οὐκ ἠδυνήθητε is taken closely with πάντων, the meaning is roughly as follows: 'Through Jesus Christ forgiveness is offered from all sins, something which the law never offered.'[1] Although grammatically feasible, it seems most unlikely that Luke intends to propound a theory of double justification – the law delivers us from some things, the gospel from others – which would be not only un-Pauline but essentially un-Lucan too (cf. Ac. 4:12; 15:11; 26:18). The looseness of Luke's statement probably results in part from his desire to duplicate Pauline language without knowing precisely how Paul used it. The assertion that the gospel provides what life under the law lacks is made solely with respect to the Christian view of salvation. It does not follow that the law has been done away with or that it no longer has a role to play in Jewish or Jewish-Christian piety; it means simply that the law, on its own, is an inadequate vehicle of salvation.

In his address to the council in Jerusalem, Peter argues against the imposition of the law upon Gentile believers for a variety of reasons, including the following: 'Now therefore why do you make trial of God by putting a yoke upon the neck of the disciples which neither our fathers nor we have been able to bear? But we believe that we shall be saved through the grace of the Lord Jesus, just as they will' (Ac. 15:10—11). The connection between verse 10 and the verses which precede (verses 7—9) and follow it (verse 11) is not too clear. The verse is commonly interpreted in isolation, as a self-contained statement which gives one of the few glimpses of Luke's real view of the law. As a Gentile Christian, that is, Luke views the law as a mass of detailed commands, intolerably oppressive and quite incapable of fulfilment.[2] If this is so Luke joins a long line of Christian writers who misunderstand the purpose of Jewish nomism and overlook the role which repentance and forgiveness play in it. As Nolland has recently argued, however, it is unlikely that Luke meant this.[3] On the one hand, strictly speaking such a view would require Luke to conclude that the law should be abandoned by Jewish as well as Gentile Christians,[4] which would scarcely be a helpful proposition in the circumstances as Luke describes them and which does not accord with the role of the law among Jewish-Christians as Luke recounts it elsewhere. On the other hand, Luke's sympathetic description of genuine legal piety and his frequent references to Jewish-Christians keeping the law make it most improbable that he believed the law was *of necessity* an impossible burden. Indeed, Nolland argues that neither ζυγός nor βαστάζειν necessarily conveys the meaning 'burdensome' and that verse 10 has nothing to do with the oppressiveness of the Jewish legal system. The first term commonly refers to an obligation which is gladly undertaken (as in the 'yoke of the law') and the second to something which requires effort rather than something resented or unwillingly borne. Taking verse 10 closely with the surrounding verses, Nolland suggests that the argument of Peter's speech has solely to do with the question of the salvation of Jews and Gentiles: lack of the law did not exclude Cornelius and his household from salvation (verses 7—9); possession of the law did not bring salvation to the Jews since they did not fulfil its demands (verse 10); Jews and Gentiles alike are saved solely by the grace of God (verse 11). It is more difficult than Nolland supposes to confine verse 10 exclusively to the issue of Jewish salvation, but it is not necessary to be persuaded at every turn to agree that verse 10 is best read in conjunction with verse 11 and that it has to do with the issue of salvation and the law which dominates the surrounding discussion (15:1, 5, 11). Nolland treats σωθῆναι as an infinitive of result — 'But through the grace of God we *believe* (in order) to be saved and so do they' — but whether we follow him in this or not the issue is, as in

13:38–9, the place of adherence to the law in the economy of salvation. In both passages, with respect to salvation, the law is seen to be inadequate, irrelevant or both. The implications for the status of the law are, from a Jewish viewpoint, profound, but Luke shows no interest in dwelling on them. In neither case does he imply that for Jewish-Christians obedience to the law is to be discouraged or abandoned. These criticisms of the law from the point of view of the Christian message of salvation find no parallel elsewhere in Acts and, if we do not read Acts through Pauline eyes, they are unemphatic. One explanation for this is that Luke held an essentially conservative view of the law and muffled any serious criticism because he believed that the Church, as the renewed Israel, was committed to keeping it.[5] A quite different explanation is to suppose that on a theological level the issue of the law was relatively unimportant for Luke and his readers.[6]

B. Keeping the law

One thing is unambiguously clear from the narrative of Acts, namely that Luke, despite his conviction that the law was an inadequate instrument of salvation, is nowhere critical of Jews or Jewish-Christians who choose to keep the law, with the possible exception of Peter in Ac. 10–11. This is apparent not only from occasional, passing allusions but most emphatically in the stories about Stephen and Paul. Indeed, it is difficult to find much of significance in Acts with regard to the question of Jewish Christians and the law except in incidents connected with these two figures.

Certainly, it is assumed by Luke that the Christians in Jerusalem worshipped in the Temple (Ac. 2:46; 3:1; 5:42) and that those in the diaspora attended the synagogues (Ac. 13:14; 14:1; 17:2). Ananias is described as a man 'devout according to the law' (Ac. 21:12), unlike his Jewish contemporaries who fail to keep the law delivered to them by angels (Ac. 7:53). These few references concur with material in Luke's Gospel (especially Lk. 1–2; 10:25f) and show that Luke wrote with the assumption that Jewish-Christians would normally keep the law, but they are a meagre collection and in many contexts keeping the law is incidental to more important themes such as the healing in Ac. 13:14f. While we should not overlook the implication of these casual allusions, it can scarcely be said that they reveal an overriding interest on Luke's part in the early Church as a law-abiding community.[7] When we turn to the narratives about Stephen and Paul, especially the latter, the law suddenly becomes a major issue. This is apparent, as noted in chapter 1, in the distribution of νόμος and related terms throughout Acts, almost all of which are connected in one way or another with Stephen and Paul. The charges against Stephen in chapter 6 are given in three different forms but accuse him of essentially the same things:

verse 11: blasphemy against Moses and God

verse 13: blasphemy against the law and this holy place

verse 14: Jesus will change the customs of Moses and destroy this place.

It is made clear that the charges are unfounded since his accusers, primed for their task by the Jewish authorities, are described as 'false witnesses' (Ac. 6:11, 13). The notorious problem of the relationship between the accusations and the speech of Stephen need not be reviewed here. It is sufficient to note that insofar as the speech does deal with the charges it does so obliquely, at best answering them by implication and allusion. Moreover, there is no mention in the speech of Jesus' relationship to the law and the Temple, which is the form the accusations take in Ac. 6:14. The question of the law is raised only twice: in Ac. 7:38 Moses is described as the recipient of 'living oracles' and in Ac. 7:53 the Jews are accused of failing to keep the law, thus throwing back at them the charge they levelled at Stephen. Moses is an important figure in other parts of the speech but more, it seems, in his role as prophet and leader than as lawgiver. These two references are not much to go on, but it can at least be said that they confirm what Luke has already made clear in the preceding narrative: Stephen is not an antinomian. In order to give this observation its full weight we must remember that for Luke, contrary to what our historical analyses commonly tell us, Stephen represents the whole Church or at least a respectable part of it.

Of the three versions of the charges against Stephen, 6:14 is certainly the most curious. It is related, as is often noted, to the charges laid against Jesus at his trial as reported in the other Gospels but not in Luke. Why in Luke's writings they appear in connection with Stephen rather than Jesus is a puzzle to which no satisfactory solution has been found,[8] unless it has to do with a change of circumstances between the writing of the Gospel and Acts such that in the interim the law had in some way become an important issue. It is perhaps worth noting that the accusation is cast in the future tense, speaking of what Jesus will do rather than what he has done (καταλύσει, ἀλλάξει). If the future tenses are taken strictly they provide us with an approximate parallel to Lk. 16:17 when that verse is read as an assertion of the abiding validity of the law. But whether we consider the future tenses to be precise or not, it would seem that for Luke's denial of the charges against Stephen to be effective he must be taken to imply that what Jesus will not do in the future he did not do in the past. Indeed, Jervell argues that in view of Ac. 6:14 we must assume that none of the material in the Gospel was understood by Luke to be critical of the law.[9] As we have seen, however, the Gospel evidence cannot be so neatly categorized, and a degree of tension remains between Ac. 6:14 and some of the Gospel evidence, especially the sabbath controversies and the divorce saying. Moreover, since the accusation in Ac. 6:14 is couched in terms of Jesus' attack on the 'customs of Moses' – a phrase which, as we have seen, can include practices which rest on written law or oral tradition – the tension with the sabbath stories would remain even if they were thought to turn on matters of scribal tradition rather than written law.

It is perhaps worth noting, too, that when Acts was written the Temple had been destroyed and, partly as a consequence of this, the law had become increasingly central to Jewish experience. Is it significant that Stephen's speech largely ignores the question of law and in its brief allusions contains no criticism of it, whereas the Temple theme is discussed critically and at some length? Is Luke instinctively avoiding conflict by taking account of current Jewish experience?

In connection with Paul the law becomes a central theme. He is repeatedly accused by hostile Jews of attacking the law (Ac. 21:28; 23:29; 24:5–6; 25:7). The charges made against him are repetitive, probably Lucan, and concern three matters: it is alleged that Paul has abandoned the law and customs, profaned the Temple and generally stirred up trouble. The reply to these accusations is complex and goes beyond the narratives in which they are specifically raised. First, they are flatly denied and perhaps nowhere more clearly than in Ac. 25:8 (cf. 24:14–15; 28:17): 'Neither against the law of the Jews, nor against the Temple, nor against Caesar have I offended at all.' This comprehensive denial unambiguously reveals Luke's conviction that Paul was innocent of all the charges laid against him, Jewish or Roman. Indeed, when the Jews attempt to interest the Roman authorities in Paul's case he is always found to be innocent of political misdemeanours and whatever disputes he has with the Jews are declared to be an internal matter of no interest to the Romans. A second way Luke asserts Paul's innocence is to deflect criticism of his view of the law by insisting that the real dispute was over the questions of resurrection and messiahship and that even then Paul parted company with only some Jews, such as the Sadducees, whereas others like the Pharisees should have found his views congenial (Ac. 23:6; 24:21; 25:18–19). The approximate identification of Paul's views with those of the Pharisees has behind it not only historical probability – in that Paul was a Pharisee and, like the early Church in general, shared much in common with them – but perhaps also Luke's recognition of the realities of post-70 Judaism. When Luke wrote the Sadducees were a spent force (and thus an easy target) while the successors of the Pharisees were extending their control over Judaism with increasing success.

The third and perhaps most startling of Luke's ploys is found in his depiction of Paul as at all times a faithful and law-abiding Jew (Ac. 16:1– 3; 18:18; 22:3–4, 12–16, 17, 21; 23:1–5; 26:4–5). In this respect Paul's behaviour is consistent and the pattern remains unbroken throughout Acts even when it strains the reader's credulity, not to mention that of the historian who knows Paul's letters. It is worth our while to dwell on a few of these stories to see how Luke achieves this effect.

In Ac. 16:1–3 Luke recounts the circumcision by Paul of Timothy, son of a Christian Jewish mother and a Gentile father, 'because of the Jews that were in those places, for they all knew that his father was a Greek' (verse 3). According to later rabbinic tradition marriage between a Jew and a non-Jew was forbidden and illegal (based on Dt. 7:1; 21:13), but the offspring of a Jewish woman and Gentile man were considered to be both Jewish and, in some cases, illegitimate too.[10] Luke seems to imply that Jews would automatically assume that the son of a Gentile would not be circumcised, though this would not necessarily have been the case. That Timothy was not circumcised may have been because his father forbad it, because his mother was a Christian, or perhaps because of a more liberal attitude towards circumcision among diaspora Jews. The crucial point for Luke, however, is that Timothy's circumcision removes a stigma that might otherwise prevent him from being an effective missionary companion to Paul when working among Jews. In terms of the Lucan world the story is plausible enough – Paul shows good tactical sense and, in terms of what we can surmise about first-century belief, encourages Timothy to do what Jews would expect him to do to confirm his Jewish identity. When the evidence of Paul's letters is introduced, however, things look rather different. The result is that the narrative is frequently dismissed as sheer fantasy, based perhaps on false and malicious rumours about Paul's practice of circumcision such as are alluded to in Gal. 5:11.[11] In view of Gal. 5:2f, the fuss over Titus' circumcision in Gal. 2, and the fact that Timothy was a baptized Christian, it is commonly held that under no circumstances could Paul have countenanced this circumcision, even as a tactical ploy, and especially if it is supposed to have occurred immediately after the apostolic council in Acts 15. To this we might add that some think that the agreement recorded in Gal. 2:9 proves that Paul never engaged in missionary work among Jews after that point. These arguments are by no means always persuasive. The case of Timothy, a Jew in Jewish eyes, is different from that of Titus the Gentile. The circumcision of Timothy is precisely the kind of event that may have given rise to the rumours of Gal. 5:11, and there is nothing in Paul's letters which precludes such behaviour in this exceptional case and for the purpose specified. It may look a little strange following on the heels of the apostolic council, but this may mean only that Luke has misplaced the incident — an argument that is also relevant if we take the unlikely view that the agreement of Gal. 2:9 remained in force from that time on. I Cor. 9:19f is rightly brought into the discussion and shows the lengths to which Paul was prepared to go in order to preach the gospel. It cannot be dismissed by Overbeck's judgement that 'the historical Paul recognises over and against the law only the Christian freedom *not* to fulfil it',[12] since this seems to ignore what Paul plainly says in I Cor. 9, the general principles he enunciates with regard to the weak and the strong (I Cor. 10), and the exceptional nature of Timothy's case which as a rule does not come into view when the status of Jews and Gentiles is discussed. Nevertheless, our purpose is not so much to come to any firm conclusions about the historical plausibility of this incident as to show that what is within Lucan terms a wholly believable story is, when assessed by evidence extraneous to Luke's narrative, open to some doubt.

According to Ac. 21:17–27 Paul, on arriving in Jerusalem, is informed by James that the many thousands of Jewish-Christians zealous for the law have heard rumours that he teaches 'all the Jews who are among the Gentiles to forsake Moses, telling them not to circumcise their children or observe the customs' (verse 21). It is assumed by the Christian leaders that the rumours are false and to prove Paul's faithfulness to the law they advise him to join four men under a Nazirite vow and pay the costs of bringing it to completion. Paul takes their advice and we must assume that Luke thought it had the required effect on the Jewish-Christians in Jerusalem even though Paul is arrested at the instigation of some Asian Jews before this can be shown. In Lucan terms the narrative is straightforward: faced with suspicion about his attitude towards the law in general, Paul agrees to a supererogatory ritual which was viewed by Jews to be a special act of piety. When assessed in the light of Paul's statement in I Cor. 9:19f there seems no reason to reject the story, although the motive of removing Jewish-Christian suspicion and proving Paul's commitment to the law, expressed by James in Ac. 21:24*b*, is rather different from his own stated motives in I Cor. 9 — 'to win those under the law' or 'for the sake of the gospel'. Certainly, there is no evidence that Paul discouraged Jewish-Christians from keeping the law if they so wished. The more problematic historical issue is to understand Paul's action in the light of Jewish evidence for Nazirite vows. As Luke relates the story it seems that Paul joins the four men in their Nazirite vow by undertaking a seven-day purity ritual at the end of which, after the appropriate offerings, both he and they will have fulfilled their obligations. The narrative seems to imply that the four men also undertook the seven-day purity rite, but this is not clear. According to evidence from Jewish sources (especially the Mishnah tractate *Nazir*) the minimum length of a Nazirite vow was thirty days (cf. Jos. *Bell.* II.313). A seven-day ritual to remove levitical impurity during a Nazirate interrupted the latter and, depending on the cause of impurity, involved either starting the Nazirate again or fulfilling the days remaining before the onset of impurity (*Nazir* 7.2—3). Paying the costs of someone else's offerings seems to have been common enough (cf. Jos. *Ant.* XIX.6.1), but otherwise it is hard to bring Luke's account into line with the Jewish evidence. Paul could not have joined in a Nazirate for less than thirty days and if the four men joined him in a seven-day ritual which also completed their Nazirate we must assume a remarkable coincidence between the onset of their impurity and Paul's arrival in Jerusalem. Stolle suggests that both Paul (cf. Ac. 18:18) and the four men had previously taken a Nazirite vow abroad, had returned to Jerusalem simultaneously and, because the Nazirite vow was valid only if fulfilled in the land of Israel, all required a seven-day purification followed by thirty further days in the Nazirate.[13] Luke, of course, does not say that the men were abroad and in Paul's case, if Ac. 18:22f does refer to a visit to Jerusalem, it is strange that his vow was not completed then. Haenchen assumes that two separate things have been confused:[14] the Nazirite vow of four Jerusalem Christians which they had completed but were too poor to conclude; and Paul's seven-day purity rite required by his sojourn abroad and his desire to participate in the ceremony completing the four men's Nazirate. Thus in reality Paul did not participate in the Nazirate and the four men did not share in the seven-day rite. Luke overlaps the two and creates the impression that all the men participated in both rites. Even Haenchen's plausible explanation involves some reading between the lines but, whether we accept this or some other explanation of the origin of Luke's version, there can be little doubt that as it stands it makes little sense in terms of current Jewish practice. This provides us with an interesting contrast to Ac. 16:1—3: there the story concurs with what we know of Jewish practice and belief and the problems arise when Paul's letters are brought into play; here there are no major obstacles in Paul, but the narrative seems confused when read in the light of Jewish evidence.

In Ac. 22:30—23:5 Luke describes Paul's appearance before the Sanhedrin. The narrative is riddled with problems. The meeting of the council is 'commanded' by the Roman tribune who then attends it himself to assess the dispute between Paul and the Jews. The sharp dispute between Paul and his accusers, in which he has the most to say even though he is the accused, is enigmatic: Paul is struck on the mouth for no apparent reason, turns the tables on his accusers by threatening them with the judgement of God and declaring their behaviour to be illegal, and when accused of reviling the High Priest he abjectly backs down with the words, 'I did not know, brethren, that he was the high priest; for it is written, "You shall not speak evil of a ruler of your people." ' Haenchen comments bluntly: 'If we read it as an historical report then the persons act very strangely and in an improbable and incomprehensible manner.'[15] It is unclear why the tribune had Paul 'bound' through the previous night (22:30), and why he is present at the meeting of the Sanhedrin even if he had the right to convene it (cf. Jos. *Ant.* XX.202).[16] No explanation is offered for the decision to strike Paul or of his somewhat excessive initial response and, above all, it seems wholly implausible to suppose that Paul would not have known that Ananias was the High Priest. To argue that Paul had poor eyesight, that the High Priest was a new incumbent or was perhaps less visible in the presence of the tribune, displays a certain air of desperation; and to suppose that Paul was being ironic is not a great deal more convincing. Quite apart from evidence that we might bring to bear on it from the outside it would take a singularly unalert reader of Acts to take this scene at its face value, especially in view of the dominant role of the High Priest in all previous gatherings of the Sanhedrin mentioned in Acts (e.g. 4:5f; 5:17f; 6:15). Yet the story, of course, has its point – to prove beyond all doubt that Paul, even in the most dire of circumstances, would never consciously break the law. When it is pointed out that he has done so unwittingly, he immediately retracts.

There are a number of things common to these three stories. They are perhaps the most explicit examples in Acts of narratives designed to prove Paul's continuing obedience to the law and sensitivity towards Jewish scruples. Equally, all three attain a degree of implausibility when viewed in the light of evidence from Paul, from Judaism, or even from within the narrative of Acts itself. Luke, it appears, knew little about Judaism and not a great deal more about Paul, but he was determined to show that at all times and in all circumstances Paul was a faithful and law-abiding Jew. The point can perhaps be made another way too. The examples we have discussed and similar incidents are usually, and rightly, considered in the light of Paul's statement in I Cor. 9:19f. The degree to which this statement can be used to justify the 'Jewishness' of Paul in Acts is open to some dispute, but it is remarkable that Luke reveals only one side of Paul's accommodation 'for the sake of the gospel', i.e. becoming a Jew to those who were Jews. Despite Luke's interest in the Gentile mission and the central role Paul performs in it, there is not a single example in Acts of Paul behaving as a Gentile to those who were Gentiles, whether 'for the sake of the gospel' or for any other reason. Even when preaching to the Gentiles Paul behaves like a Jew. To put things in this way, as to use other forms of historical information to assess his narrative, is to depart from our main aim, which is to read Luke's narrative as he presents it. But it merely dramatizes what is already evident in those narratives themselves: Paul is without exception a law-abiding Jew. One obvious conclusion to draw is that zeal for the law was viewed by Luke as in no way incompatible with Christian belief. But in view of the dominance of the figure of Paul when the law is at issue in Acts, and the unbroken portrait which results, we might well wonder whether the real issue for Luke was not the law *per se*, but Paul. Was it the contentious reputation of Paul, perhaps under fire from Jewish-Christian quarters, which led Luke to deal with the problem of the law at such length and with such anxiety when prior to this it does not seem to have concerned him much at all?

C. Law and Gentiles

The status of the law among Gentile Christians is the main topic in two closely related stories — the conversion of Cornelius and the apostolic council. The details of both stories are often obscure and the connection between them is puzzling, but some attempt must be made to understand them if we are to grasp Luke's overall view of the law. If Luke was writing primarily for Gentile Christians, as much of our discussion has so far indicated, his view of the role of the law among Gentiles would be the one aspect of the broader theme of law which would be of immediate practical significance to his readers. It may be, too, that his view of this matter indirectly sheds light on his estimation of the status of the law among Jewish Christians.

The story of Cornelius' conversion raises at least three significant points about the law:

(1) Peter's vision, which ostensibly deals with the dissolution of the distinction between clean and unclean foods (Lev. 11), is interpreted by him as signifying the dissolution of the similar, but not identical, distinction between clean and unclean people (Ac. 10:28–9). Indeed, many have supposed that the confusion of these two matters arises because Luke reinterprets a traditional account of Peter's vision for the purposes of his own narrative. This may be so, but it is clear that the two issues were readily connected,[17] since one of the chief things which made Gentiles, and any Jew who ate with them, unclean was the consumption of unclean

food – and this is presumably the point of the accusation that Peter had mixed with the uncircumcised and eaten with them (Ac. 11:3 cf. 10:48).

What, if anything, we are supposed to infer about the question of clean and unclean animals is unclear. Peter does not in fact 'kill and eat' as he is commanded in the vision and, had he done so, presumably he could have chosen a clean rather than an unclean animal from those available. If the vision implies that the levitical distinction between clean and unclean has been revoked then a radical departure from the Torah is clearly implied. Luke, however, does not pursue this matter because he understands the vision primarily as a sort of parable about the problem of mixing and eating with unclean people. Peter, presented here as a scrupulously law-abiding Jew, is required by the vision to act 'illegally': 'You yourselves know how illegal (ἀθέμιτος) it is for a Jew to associate with or to visit anyone of another nation (κολλᾶσθαι ἢ προσέρχεσθαι ἀλλοφύλῳ).' The force of ἀθέμιτος is not clear. It refers basically to an action which defies the divine order (θέμις) of the universe rather than the law (νόμος). Thus it can refer generally to anything which is 'godless' or 'abominable' (I Pet. 4:3; Did. 16:4; I Clem. 63:2; II Macc. 10:34; Jos. *Bell.* I.84, 659; VI.209) but it is frequently used to describe an act contradictory to Jewish law (II Macc. 7:1; Jos. *Bell.* I.650; II.131; IV.99, 205; *Vit.* 26; *Ap.* II.119), the clearest example of which is found in II Macc. 6:5: τοῖς ἀποδιεσταλμένοις ἀπὸ τῶν νόμων ἀθεμίτοις. If by ἀθέμιτος Luke means something contrary to Jewish law then clearly he thought that one part of the law had been overturned, namely the distinction between clean and unclean people which caused the social segregation of Jews and Gentiles. That there is no such distinction in the Torah which applied to all Jews everywhere and that there is no evidence that this was thought to be the case within all Jewish groups before 70 C.E., would mean that Luke was mistaken insofar as 10:28 is presented as a statement about all Jews. There is, of course, ample evidence from both Jewish and Classical sources that many Jews believed it necessary to separate themselves from Gentiles (Philo *Spec. Leg.* I.51; *Virt.* 175; *Migr. Abr.* 89f; Jos. *Ant.* XIV.199–265; *Ap.* II.190–219; Sib. Or. 3:592f; Dio Cass. XXXVII.17.1f; Tac. *Hist.* V.5.4; S.B. IV.353f) and according to Sevenster the fundamental objection to Judaism in the Classical world concerned the reluctance of the Jews to mix with others.[18] Separation from the Gentiles also involved avoidance of their food (Dan. 1:8; Jud. 12:1–4; Tob. 1:10–11; II Macc. 6, 7; Esth. 4:17 LXX; III Macc. 3:4; 7:11; Jos. *Ant.* IV.137; *Vit.* 14; Jos. and As. 7:1; Jub. 2:16–18). However, it should not be forgotten that this evidence refers to Jewish practice and not to Torah legislation and that it is not even certain that before 70 C.E. it was believed that the levitical rules of purity were of any relevance to Gentiles at all.[19] Moreover, it is doubtful that separation from non-Jews, including a refusal to eat with them, was universally practised by all Jews in this period.[20] In other words, Luke may have assumed that the practice of some Jews was a law for all Jews and, if so, it may be because the form of Judaism known to him had been increasingly influenced by the rabbinic programme for levitical purity after 70 C.E. However, this would not reduce the force of the observation that Luke thought that God had intervened to abrogate part of the law. In view of the paradigmatic significance of this narrative for Luke it seems unlikely that he thought that this was relevant to Peter alone; rather, it would appear to apply to all Jewish-Christians, or at least to those engaged in missionary work among Gentiles.

If on the other hand we suppose that Luke deliberately chose ἀθέμιτος rather than the more specific ἄνομος precisely because it had a more general meaning, it may express his awareness that the distinction between clean and unclean was seen to be part of the order of things, a matter of ingrained custom and practice, rather than the result of a legal prescription. If so, then the effect of the vision is not to contravene the law as such but to challenge what Luke knew to be the common Jewish practice of segregation from Gentiles. Certainly it contradicts the view of the Jamnian sages and what was probably the view of pre-70 Pharisaism as well as the practice of many other Jews, but the law as such is not at stake. If this is what Luke means then what is otherwise the only incident in Acts where Jews or Jewish-Christians are discouraged from keeping their law disappears and we are left with a uniform picture. If not, then it serves by way of contrast to emphasize the remarkable consistency of Luke's portrait of Paul as a law-abiding Jew, and it is of some interest that it is Peter rather than Paul who is allowed the one break with Jewish legal tradition.

(2) Peter gives his own summary of the significance of the Cornelius episode in the following words: 'In every nation he that fears him and works righteousness (ὁ φοβούμενος αὐτὸν καὶ ἐργαζόμενος δικαιοσύνην) is acceptable to him' (Ac. 10:35). It is a conclusion which is obviously appropriate to the pious Cornelius, described earlier in precisely these terms: 'a devout man who feared God (εὐσεβὴς καὶ φοβούμενος τὸν θεόν) with all his household, gave alms liberally and prayed constantly to God' (10:2) and an 'upright and godfearing man' (ἀνὴρ δίκαιος καὶ φοβούμενος τὸν θεόν 10:22). At the same time it is remarkably similar to diaspora-Jewish summaries of the law and, although presented as part of Peter's Christian experience, expresses no more than what we might call a 'liberal' Jewish position.[21] A tendency to summarize the law in terms of belief in

One God together with a few basic ethical demands was widespread in diaspora Judaism. Philo *Spec. Leg.* II.62–3 is a particularly apt example since it refers to the weekly synagogue meetings in each city, which were open to the public at large, and summarizes the teaching that went on there into two main themes: 'But among the vast number of particular truths and principles studied, there stands out so to speak, high above the others two main heads: one of duty to God as shown by piety and holiness (εὐσέβεια, ὁσιότης), one of duty to men as shown by humanity and justice (φιλανθρωπία, δικαιοσύνη), each of them splitting up into multiform branches, all highly laudable.'[22] The contrast between conservative Palestinian and liberal diaspora attitudes can be seen in the story of the conversion of King Izates (Jos. *Ant.* XX.34–48) – even though we should probably not draw sweeping conclusions about the differences between Palestinian and diaspora Judaism on the basis of this story alone. Summaries of the law in terms of its central demands are precisely what we also find in Lk. 10:25; 11:42. The effect of the vision is thus that Peter abandons his conservative (Palestinian?) position for a more liberal (diaspora-Jewish and Christian?) stance.

(3) The most perplexing issue is the relationship between Ac. 10–11 and the discussion of Gentile obligation to the law in Ac. 15. The reader is specifically invited to connect the two in Ac. 15:7–9, where the conversion of Cornelius is recalled and used as one reason for the decision not to require circumcision of Gentile converts. We have on the one hand to decide why the problem of the Gentiles and the law is reopened in chapter 15 when it had apparently been settled in chapters 10–11, and on the other hand to explain the even more curious relationship between the terms of the apostolic decree and the conclusions reached about the status of Gentiles on the basis of Cornelius' conversion. The first problem arises because Ac. 11:18 looks remarkably like a unanimous recognition by the Jerusalem Christians of the acceptability of Gentiles without circumcision and the law. On hearing Peter's account the Jerusalem leaders, including presumably 'those from the circumcision' (11:2), are silenced and recognize that 'to the Gentiles God has granted repentance leading to life' (i.e. salvation). And yet it is precisely the issue of Gentile salvation and its connection with circumcision and obedience to the law which sparks off the controversy which the apostolic council attempts to resolve. Secondly, Peter's recognition not only that God accepts without partiality Gentiles who 'fear God and act righteously' but that he could do the same and mix and eat freely with them, appears to be forgotten when in the apostolic decree, as it is commonly understood, certain levitical obligations are required of Gentile Christians in order to resolve the question of their

relationship with Jewish Christians. The issue is the same, but in Ac. 15 it seems to be resolved in a quite different manner.[23]

A number of observations might be made with respect to the first of these matters. It might be argued, for example, that the Cornelius incident is in a number of ways exceptional. Peter's vision is unique and perhaps prompted him to take an approach to Gentiles which did not immediately become normative.[24] Equally it might be argued that Cornelius, whom Luke is at pains to describe as a particularly pious Gentile, was also exceptional and what was appropriate in his case was not necessarily appropriate for all Gentile believers. Perhaps, moreover, Cornelius and his household were such a small number that they did not pose the same problems as a much larger influx of Gentiles not all of whom were godfearers. Or again, it might be noted that the primary issue in chapters 10–11 is the initial contact of Jewish-Christians with Gentiles for the purpose of preaching, whereas in chapter 15 the problem is how to regulate Gentile Christian behaviour after they have joined the Church. Yet while such observations are not wholly without value they do not finally resolve the issue. Thus not only is Peter's experience referred to in 15:7–11 as in some sense normative, but also in that passage, as throughout chapters 10–11, there is a constant shifting between Cornelius in particular and the Gentiles in general, such that the former is clearly representative of the latter (10:34, 45; 11:17–18). While for Luke Cornelius' conversion is in some senses exceptional, much more important is its paradigmatic significance. What applies to Cornelius applies to all Gentiles and decisions made in his regard establish principles appropriate to them all. Moreover, the conclusion of 11:17–18 that the Gentiles have received the 'Spirit and life' (i.e. salvation) is directly challenged by the manner in which the issue of circumcision is raised in 15:1 (cf. verse 5) — 'Unless you are circumcised according to the customs of Moses you cannot be saved'. The issue in chapter 15 is thus not merely post-conversion behaviour but what constitutes true conversion in the first place. The Gentiles referred to in 15:1, 5 are presumably those converted as a result of the mission of Paul and Barnabas in chapters 13–14. Most of them, like Cornelius, were probably thought to be godfearers, although the fluidity of Luke's terminology does not make this clear in each case.[25] In 13:43 they are described by the curious term οἱ σεβόμενοι προσήλυτοι, probably meaning 'godfearers' (cf. verses 16, 26). The 'Greeks' of 14:1, according to the context, are probably to be seen as godfearers and are at any rate already associated with the synagogue, although the 'Gentiles' of 13:46–8 may well have included those with no previous contact with Judaism (cf. 13:44, 'the whole city gathered to hear them'). That we are to see an influx of Gentiles who were not godfearers as the reason why the question of the law is reopened in chapter 15 is still, however, improbable – not only because Luke so clearly presents Cornelius as a paradigmatic Gentile but also because we know that from a Jewish viewpoint godfearers, unlike proselytes, *were* Gentiles. They had no hybrid status, as if they were semi-proselytes, and were treated in all respects as Gentiles.

Perhaps a more fruitful explanation of the narrative tension lies elsewhere, namely in the observation that those who raise the matter of Gentile circumcision in Ac. 15 are described as a group of extreme Jewish-Christians – assuming that 'the believers from the party of the Pharisees' in 15:5 are the same as those who travelled to Antioch with the demand of circumcision (15:1) – whose demands are firmly rejected and who, in this sense, turn out to be in a minority among the Christians in Jerusalem. If οἱ ἐκ περιτομῆς in 11:2 are the same minority (as distinct from the 'apostles and brethren' of 11:1) then we might assume that their silence in 11:18 was temporary and tactical and/or that they were subsequently boosted by an influx of converts from among the Pharisees and felt confident enough to raise the matter again. If οἱ ἐκ περιτομῆς refers to the whole Jerusalem leadership,[26] then we might assume that the influx of newly converted Pharisees was sufficient in Luke's mind to explain the reopening of a problem that had already been resolved to the satisfaction of the Jerusalem leaders.

Far more difficult to explain is the decision in chapter 15 to impose certain minimum demands upon Gentile converts. It is clear that adherence to the law is seen to be of no significance for salvation, but it is strange not only that demands other than 'fearing God and acting righteously' are imposed but also that these consist in the main of food rules to regulate social intercourse between Jewish and Gentile Christians. What then of Peter's view that his vision had established a new basis for Jewish and Gentile communion? Haenchen comments as follows: 'In the Cornelius story Luke admittedly could not have brought in the four prohibitions, but it is obvious that the centurion's piety could have accommodated them.'[27] Haenchen correctly notes that the terms of the decree would be out of place in the Cornelius narrative, but his reference to Cornelius' accommodating piety is beside the point. Doubtless a pious godfearer could be prevailed upon to concede these, and indeed many other, demands; but the issue at stake is not the piety but the status of Gentiles *vis à vis* the law. Moreover, such an interpretation ignores the paradigmatic significance of Cornelius in Luke's scheme of things. Haenchen's view might perhaps be adapted and extended. If, for example, Ac. 10:35 is taken to be a precise and technical reference to godfearers rather than a general comment on Gentile piety, and if we assume that it was in fact the case, or that Luke believed it to be so, that godfearers normally abstained from those things prohibited by the decree, the tension between Ac. 10–11 and Ac. 15 would be considerably reduced. The decree would simply be confirming those practices common among godfearers and requiring them of Gentile Christians with no previous contact with Judaism. There is, however, no evidence that this was the case or that Luke thought it to be so. In fact we know nothing about the regulations for godfearers in first-century Judaism. The requirements which come closest and which might have been in force, the Noachic laws, are dissimilar in both number and content to the terms of the decree.[28] They do not, for example, forbid the consumption of 'things sacrificed to idols', although this might be subsumed under the general prohibition of idolatry, and it is the shedding rather than the consumption of blood which is banned.

A somewhat different tack is taken by O'Neill, whose ambivalence on the matter can be seen in the following quotation:

> Nevertheless, we can maintain that there is no formal contradiction between Peter's vision and the terms of the decree: the distinction between clean and unclean could have been abolished and the restrictions of the decree enforced at the same time. Of course the spirit of Peter's vision was lost once the Church started to make cultic regulations regarding food, but perhaps it was possible that the practical and tactical reasons for the regulations may not have been felt to count against the general import of the vision. The fact that the vision was used to adorn the principle that Gentiles were to be admitted to the body of believers on equal terms with the Jews is evidence that the vision lived on, although the practical consequences that should have flowed from it were being eroded.[29]

O'Neill reaches this conclusion on the basis of a series of observations which, it should be noted, are more concerned with unravelling the sources and events which underlie Luke's narrative than with the internal coherence of that narrative itself. Thus he considers it doubtful that the issue of table-fellowship had to be settled before Gentile Christians could be admitted to congregations and likely that Cornelius would have known how to entertain a Jew without giving offence. He thinks that the terms of the decree are designed to facilitate the sharing of common meals by Jewish and Gentile Christians by ensuring not only that forbidden foods were not offered to Jews but that Gentiles were not polluted by their own use of them. Pollution is the basis for banning πορνεία too and O'Neill takes it to refer to marriage within the forbidden degrees.[30] As an analysis of the historical probabilities O'Neill's suggestions are not always convincing. It might be argued, for example, that the terms of the decree are as incompatible with the declaration that all foods are clean as with the saying attributed to Jesus that 'it is not what goes into a man which defiles him but what comes out' (Mk 7:15). To consider them compatible requires a precise distinction between meat that was unclean because it came from forbidden animals (Lev. 11) and that which was unclean because of its place of origin or mode of preparation (Lev. 17).[31] It is difficult to imagine why this distinction would have been made in the context of Jew—Gentile relations — which is presumably the context to which Peter's vision, if it has any historical basis, belongs. Why should it have been supposed, for example, that pork and blood, equally abhorrent to a Jew and both unequivocally prohibited by the law, should be treated differently? To distinguish between things unclean by association (the decree) and those unclean by declaration (various foods) makes some sense for εἰδωλόθυτα and πορνεία, but not for αἷμα / πνικτός. But quite apart from their plausibility on a historical level, O'Neill's suggestions shed little light on the way Luke tells the story. For the same reason the common and convincing observation that Luke has exaggerated the significance of Cornelius' conversion is of little assistance.[32] Even if O'Neill is right in supposing that Peter's vision and the terms of the decree are logically compatible, this does little to resolve the tension in Luke's narrative in which it is precisely consequences for social mixing and common meals which he considers to be the main import of the vision. Thus the tension which O'Neill senses even on a historical level — the loss of the 'spirit' of Peter's vision, etc. — is in fact exacerbated in Luke's version of events.

Another suggestion is to suppose that while the issue of table-fellowship is dealt with in chapters 10—11 the decree deals with the scruples of Jewish-Christians which created a barrier to all forms of relationship with Gentile Christians.[33] It does not return to the topic of table-fellowship, for which its few rules would at any rate be inadequate,[34] but deals more generally with the *modus vivendi* of Jewish and Gentile Christians and perhaps especially with conditions which would facilitate common worship. Again, while there may be some merit to this suggestion as an explanation of the original purpose of the decree, it does not explain why, according to Luke, not only eating but also social mixing with Gentiles resulted from Peter's vision. The effect of the decree would then be to revoke the decision of chapter 11 that the Gentiles were to be considered clean, since the Jewish objection to εἰδωλόθυτα, αἷμα, etc. was precisely that they polluted both those who ate them and those with whom the eaters subsequently came into contact. Quite apart from this it is difficult to imagine how Luke could have supposed that the question of common meals was settled without reference to the broader issue, since the former is an example – and perhaps the most troublesome one – of the latter, so that the resolution of the one would imply the resolution of the other. It might have been possible to allow social mixing and common worship without participation in common meals, but for anyone with even a minimal knowledge of Judaism the reverse would have made no sense.

The preceding discussion has been predicated on a particular understanding of the decree, namely that it concerns prohibitions, mainly concerned with food, which were thought to have a basis in Mosaic law. This is by far the most common understanding of the decree – so much so that it has in recent years become an *opinio communis.* The purpose of our discussion so far has been to show that when such a view is attributed to Luke it creates tensions with chapters 10–11 which cannot readily be resolved. Indeed, the tension is such that it provides us with good reason to ask whether this really was the way Luke understood the decree.

With regard to Luke's view of the Gentiles and the law the decree constitutes the nub of the problem. There is little doubt that the result of the apostolic council according to Luke was the rejection of the extremist demand that Gentile Christians should be circumcised and keep all the laws of Moses. They are, however, required to fulfil certain other obligations which are commonly understood to be a summary of the rules for 'strangers in the land' in Lev. 17–18. Gentile Christians are thus required to observe those parts of the law applicable to them, and it is misleading to speak of a 'law-free' Gentile mission because it was never the intention of the law itself that Gentiles should observe any more than these few rules.

We are thus obliged to consider the terms of the decree in more detail – a task which we can approach only with a certain diffidence. It raises notoriously complex problems of both text and interpretation and it is as unlikely that any solution will gain universal approval as it is that any individual will be fully convinced that his own views are correct. It will be simplest to consider in turn the three interpretations of the decree which have been accorded some plausibility and assess their implications for Luke's view of the role of the law among Gentile believers. Before this, however, it is worth making a few preliminary observations:

(1) Discussion of the apostolic decree has understandably been dominated by questions about its original setting and meaning in the apostolic age. For our purposes, however, the question is a different one, namely its

meaning for Luke and his readers. This distinction sounds simple enough and to some extent it has been maintained — as for example when Paul's association with the decree, which is important for Luke, is dismissed as unhistorical on the basis of the epistles. By and large, however, when the question of the text and meaning of the decree has been discussed it has been assumed that whatever seems to be the most plausible historical reconstruction can be ascribed to Luke too. It is important to disentangle these two lines of enquiry because, although many of the issues and arguments apply equally well to both, they are by no means identical. Thus we must leave open the possibility that Luke's version of the decree was different from the original or, if it was the same, that he understood it differently from those who originally devised it. We can, moreover, call upon the narrative context in which Luke places the decree to provide an indication of how he understood it in a manner denied to us when discussing its original meaning. This allows us not only to scrutinize the various terms used to refer to the decree by Luke but also to consider its broader narrative setting. Indeed, the question of the internal coherence of Luke's narrative is a matter of some significance. The rule of thumb commonly used in discussing textual variants and often adapted for the purposes of historical analysis — that the more difficult or obscure version is more likely to be original — has to be balanced on a literary level by the principle of coherence. That is, if a particular understanding of the decree coincides with a view which Luke expresses elsewhere, for example in Ac. 10−11, this may provide us with an important clue to his understanding of it even though it may be of little use in uncovering the events that lie behind his narrative.

(2) The manner in which the issue has been formulated so far contains one important presupposition: that a decree was promulgated by the leaders of the Jerusalem Church some time in the apostolic era. This I believe to be so, although who was present, what it meant and for whom it was intended are all matters which have not been finally settled and are only indirectly related to our discussion. For example, that Paul was absent when the decree was devised, that it was intended initially for a limited number of mixed congregations in Antioch, Syria and Cilicia — and was perhaps drawn up between the meeting described in Gal. 2:1−10 and the dispute in Gal. 2:11f[35] — and that it was taken to Corinth by Jewish-Christians or Paul and sparked off several of the issues discussed in I Corinthians,[36] are all fairly common reconstructions of the history of the decree and have much to be said for them, but they require no further discussion here. However, it is worth noting one consequence of the assumption that the

decree was apostolic in origin: because it was an ecclesiastical ruling which affected the everyday lives of believers and because it was considered at least by the time Luke wrote (and probably well before) to apply to all Gentile Christians, the decree presumably enjoyed wide circulation in both oral and written form and may have been subject to variation from an early stage. There is clear textual evidence that this happened at a later stage and we should probably not go far wrong to suppose it happened earlier as well. This complicates any discussion of the variant forms of the decree. On the one hand, extant variations may be products of a long and complex history. On the other hand, because of its peculiar status as an ecclesiastical ruling enjoying wide circulation independently of Acts, it may not be governed by the normal rules for assessing 'Neutral' and 'Western' readings.

(3) The problem of the text of the decree is usually considered to turn on a choice between the majority Neutral reading which includes πνικτός and the minority Western reading which omits πνικτός and adds the negative form of the golden rule.[37] Recent discussion of the text of Acts has left us with no firm guidelines which can be applied to all readings at all times. The problem is, in part, that we can no longer speak confidently of *the* Western text or *the* Neutral text or of one or the other dominating a particular locality. Both major forms circulated early and concurrently in the same areas and in different recensions. Klijn concludes the second volume of his survey of studies of the Western text with the assertion that 'the riddle of the Western text has not been solved'. Since the Western text is not a clearcut recension we have to judge each reading on its merits using the so-called 'eclectic' method. Even this provides us with no greater certainty: 'Admitting to the soundness of this procedure we nevertheless have to say that this method arrives at such varying results that we wonder whether the editors of Greek texts and translations can safely follow this road. The subjective element plays too great a part as soon as we have to judge variant readings on internal grounds alone.'[38] Although close to a counsel of despair, this conclusion obliges us to consider all readings as potentially original and to muster as many arguments as possible to settle individual cases.

With respect to the apostolic decree we can with some confidence delete the golden rule as inappropriate to the manner in which Luke presents the terms of the decree: they are things which Gentile believers should 'avoid' (ἀπέχεσθαι, διατηρεῖν ἑαυτούς, φυλάσσεθαι αὐτούς). If so, the argument commonly runs, the absence of πνικτός is not an independent variant to be discussed in its own right but is the direct result of the introduction of the golden rule.[39] This is a plausible but not a certain conclusion. It is true that if the text of the decree known to the Western editors contained πνικτός, and if the addition of the golden rule was designed to control or reflect the other terms in an ethical direction, then the deletion of πνικτός would be required. But if the version known to them did not contain πνικτός, the addition of the golden rule is quite understandable as a means of interpreting or expanding the threefold decree. In this regard it is perhaps worth noting that the Western texts omit πνικτός in Ac. 21:25 but do not include the golden rule. The once common arguments for the privileged status of the so-called 'Western non-interpolations', of which πνικτός is an example, have recently been challenged as a result of the discovery of P75;[40] but insofar as this challenge has been persuasive, it merely disallows the attribution of special merit to 'non-interpolations' and by no means removes them from contention altogether.

The observation that a shift from a 'cultic' to an 'ethical' form of the decree is more understandable than the reverse is of more weight when the original rather than the Lucan setting of the decree is being considered, although in either case it can easily lead to an over-simplified view of things. The very distinction between cultic and ethical, while convenient as a shorthand way of referring to different versions of the decree, can introduce more confusion than illumination into the discussion. In early Judaism and Christianity the two concepts were intimately related — as can be seen, for example, in the term πορνεία, however it is understood.[41] Nevertheless, whatever precise labels we choose, if we presuppose that the choice is limited to two forms of the decree, those found in the Neutral and Western texts, it makes sense to argue that the former was transformed into the latter when the problem of Jew—Gentile relations no longer existed and the reasons for the original regulations were no longer understood. The usual assumption would be that the omission of πνικτός, the term which forces a more 'cultic' reading of the decree, is directly related to the introduction of the golden rule — although even this does not preclude the possibility that πνικτός was added as a gloss to the original decree prior to the Western emendation. If this was not the case, however, and a threefold form was known to the Western editors, the addition of the golden rule would have had the effect of removing an ambiguity from, rather than radically altering the sense of, the decree — since the three terms εἰδωλόθυτα, πορνεία, αἷμα alone could be understood in a 'cultic' or an 'ethical' manner. We would then have to assume that at some stage πνικτός was added to an originally threefold decree and had the effect of resolving the ambiguity in the other direction.[42] Admittedly, it is difficult to think of reasons why πυκτός should have been added to the decree at a later date, but it is not a great deal easier to understand why this obscure term was there in the first place. Yet even if we concede the force of the argument in favour of an originally 'cultic' decree we cannot assume that Luke recorded the original text or understood the original intention of the decree. He may have recorded a threefold version and understood it 'ethically' while either a threefold or fourfold version circulated separately, was understood 'cultically', and subsequently influenced the Neutral text. If there *was* an apostolic decree, we need not suppose that Luke was the only one to record and interpret it.

A related observation is often introduced, namely that it would have been superfluous to promulgate by the decree a few ethical principles which would have been self-evident to Gentile Christians. Again the force of the argument is greater when applied to the original rather than the Lucan setting of the decree, for it is clear that an 'ethical' form of the decree would not only remove many of the tensions otherwise created with Ac. 10–11 but would also coincide with the occasions when Luke, in a manner reminiscent of hellenistic Judaism, summarizes the law into a few basic commands.[43] Moreover, it could well be argued that even in a Palestinian Jewish or early Christian environment such a decree would not have been out of place. Not only are there several examples elsewhere in the New Testament of much the same thing (cf. especially Rev. 22:15),[44] but there is the rabbinic tradition which considers the three primary sins of the Gentiles to be precisely idolatry, shedding of blood and immorality.[45] The latter is, of course, difficult to date but it may well reflect an established view of the non-Jewish world which had its roots in the first century.

It has been suggested that the change from the Neutral to the Western form of the decree is but one example of a distinct anti-Jewish tendency in the Western text, especially Codex Bezae.[46] The anti-Jewish strain, however, appears to be more an exaggeration of what is already present in the Neutral text than a distinctive tendency and to be balanced by an occasional example of pro-Jewishness and Semitic style,[47] so that it is not clear that this argument is in itself decisive for establishing the text of the decree. For what it is worth we might also bear in mind the significance of Klijn's concluding speculations about Western readings. He tentatively suggests, particularly with regard to the Gospels, that Western readings evolved in predominantly Jewish-Christian communities where oral tradition was still alive; and in order to explain the early dissemination of such readings he suggests that they go back to an important early Christian centre, namely Antioch.[48] If there is anything to these speculations and if they are thought to apply to the Western text of Acts as well, it would create a presumption in favour of the Western text of the decree, since it is improbable that a Christian community with a significant Jewish element in one of the places to which the original decree was probably addressed would have altered an originally 'cultic' decree into an 'ethical' one. If anything, quite the reverse would be expected. Clearly, however, we can do no more with these speculations than add them to the collection of puzzling data concerning the editing and transmission of New Testament documents in the first two centuries.

The result of this brief review of some of the standard arguments used to decide the text of the decree can be stated briefly: not only are many of the arguments themselves subject to uncertainty but they are of much less significance when we are searching for the Lucan, rather than the original, text of the decree. Another kind of evidence which may help at this point consists of the hints scattered through Luke's own narrative, and it is to these that we now turn.

(4) It is one of the oddities of Luke's narrative that he does not tell us precisely what the decree was for nor what it meant. We must assume that this was sufficiently well-known to his readers that it did not have to be spelled out. A number of things are, however, implicit in his presentation. The decree is connected with a debate over the imposition of the Jewish law on Gentile converts. Those who defend the view that obedience to the law was essential for the salvation of Gentile Christians are defeated and their views refuted. The majority agree that the Gentiles should not be subject to the whole law and, above all, that their relationship to the law has no bearing on their ultimate salvation. Nevertheless they are required to fulfil a few obligations, presented to them as an apostolic edict. While addressed initially to a limited number of Churches (Ac. 15:23), the decree was clearly seen by Luke as applicable to all Gentile Christians (Ac. 16:4) at all times, including his own day (Ac. 21:25, addressed to the reader). The decree is seen by the Gentile Christians as in no sense oppressive or excessively burdensome (Ac. 15:10, 19); indeed it receives an enthusiastic welcome among the Gentiles to whom it is first sent (Ac. 15:30–1). So much is clear. The central issue for our purposes is whether Luke saw the decree as the application of Torah legislation, albeit in minimal form, to Gentile Christians, thus defining once and for all their relationship to the law. There are a number of obscure hints which we must explore:

(*a*) In Ac. 15:20 Luke describes the decree in the following manner: ἀλλὰ ἐπιστεῖλαι αὐτοῖς τοῦ ἀπέχεσθαι τῶν ἀλισγημάτων τῶν εἰδώλων καὶ τῆς πορνείας καὶ τοῦ πνικτοῦ καὶ τοῦ αἵματος. The phrase ἀλισγήματα τῶν εἰδώλων replaces εἰδωλόθυτα in 15:29; 21:25 and is thought by many to be Luke's reformulation of the 'official' text of the decree as recorded in 15:29. It is probable that ἀλίσγημα qualifies εἴδωλον alone, although it may qualify the other terms too. More important is the understanding of the decree it conveys whether applied to one or all of the terms. Lake, for example, suggests that it implies ritual rather than moral pollution and may thus indicate the author's understanding of the decree.[49] Both this term and the related verb ἀλισγεῖν are rare. A ritual sense is implied in Dan. 1:8 LXX when Daniel refuses to 'defile himself' with the king's food and drink, and in Mal. 1:7, 12 which condemn priests who 'pollute' God's altar by using blemished animals for sacrifices. In Sir. 40:29, on the other hand, it has a strongly moral sense when used of a man's soul being 'polluted' by begging for or coveting another's food. This shows how easily the shift from a ritual to a moral sense can occur and that this distinction itself may not make a great deal of sense. Given the distinction, however, it is clear that the term ἀλίσγημα does not exclude an 'ethical' interpretation of the decree, and it is equally clear that if it refers to εἴδωλον alone, or if all the terms of the decree are to be connected with the activities of pagan cults, the 'cultic' sense would be entirely appropriate.

(*b*) The terms of the decree are described in Ac. 15:28 as 'necessary things' (ἐπάναγκες). This is also a rare term, usually an adverb, and the unique use here with the definite article has led to emendations.[50] More important is the sense conveyed since, whatever the syntax, it is applied to the terms of the decree by those who devised them. The basic meaning of ἐπάναγκες and cognate terms is 'obligation', frequently of a financial kind. Sometimes the obligation seems to be legal or semi-legal, as in Demosthenes *Orat.* XXXIV.7. The same may be true of Jos. *Ant.* XVI.365, though when he describes the obligation as πάτριον νόμον he may still be referring to custom rather than law in the stricter sense. Ἐπάναγκες also seems to refer to the demands of custom, as in Aeschines *Orat.* I.24 and probably Herodotus I.82 too. The papyrological evidence is often obscure and ambiguous, but appears to show a similar range of meaning, with the emphasis on local rule or custom.[51] The word thus indicates that Luke saw the terms of the decree as obligations, but it does not indicate whether they are obligations with the force of law or with the weight of custom.

(*c*) Jervell claims that φυλάσσω (Ac. 16:4; 21:25) and διατηρέω (Ac. 15:29) are technical terms in the LXX and the New Testament for 'keeping the law'.[52] This is perhaps more true of the former than the latter,[53] though both are used in a more general sense. It should be noted that two of the examples are cast in the form 'keep yourselves/themselves from'

(15:29; 21:25) while the third is related specifically to the δόγματα of the apostles and elders in Jerusalem (16:4). Indeed the term δόγμα itself can be used of the law (III Macc. 1:3; Jos. *Ap.* I.42). This does not mean, however, that the use of φυλάσσω / διατηρέω or of δόγμα means that the decree is seen as the expression of Torah. The δόγμα of 16:4 is more like the Imperial δόγμα of Lk. 2:1 (cf. Ac. 17:7) and even if we accept that φυλάσσω / διατηρέω are technical terms, which is not certain, it could be that they are designed to elevate apostolic decisions to the level of Torah rather than to present them as the expression of Torah.

(*d*) In Ac. 15:28 the apostles declare that they will place upon the Gentiles 'no greater burden (βάρος) than these necessary things'. This might be taken to suggest that the obligations of the decree could be viewed as burdensome by some Gentile Christians and some would connect it with the statement in Ac. 15:10 that the demands of the Torah were, for Jews and Jewish-Christians, something they were unable to 'bear' (βαστάζειν).[54] Yet it is not certain that 15:10 and 15:28 should be read together, in such a way that the 'burden' of verse 28 is equated with the 'things difficult to bear' in verse 10 (i.e. Mosaic laws), nor is it clear that verse 10 implies that the law was burdensome for Jews.[55] Whatever sense of 'burden' is implied by verse 28 (and is it any more than 'obligation'?) must be mitigated by the statement in 15:19 that 'we should not trouble (παρενοχλέω) the Gentiles who turn to God'. In itself Ac. 15:28 tells us neither in what sense the decree might be seen as a burden nor what connection it has, if any, with Mosaic teaching.

(*e*) It is precisely this last matter which is addressed in the notoriously obscure verse in Ac. 15:21: 'For (γάρ) from early generations Moses has had in every city those who preach him (τοὺς κηρύσσοντας) for he is read every sabbath in the synagogues.' Since the connecting γάρ is, as often in Luke—Acts, rather vague, it is not clear to what preceding statement this refers. Some connect it with the 'quotation' from Amos 9:11—12 in verses 16—18,[56] and see it as justifying the use of the prophecy as evidence that God always intended to call a nation to himself from the Gentiles; while others connect it to verse 19 and see it as an attempt to explain that the decision not to require Gentiles to keep the law in no way threatens the legitimate preaching of the law to the Jews in the synagogues.[57] The first of these seems improbable and the second, while more plausible, requires taking verses 19—20 as a single statement and supposing that verse 21 refers back only to the first part of it (leaving verse 20 in parenthesis). This creates a disjointed, but not impossible, logic. It is on the whole more natural to connect verse 21 with the verse which immediately precedes it, so that the 'preaching' in the synagogues is a justification for imposing the terms of the decree on Gentile Christians.[58] Before defining this more closely we should perhaps consider the term κηρύσσω. It is in Luke–Acts predominantly a Christian term, having as subject Jesus (Lk. 4:18–19, 44; 8:1) or Christians (Ac. 8:5; 9:20; 10:42; 19:13; 20:35; 28:31; a healed man in Lk. 8:39 and John the Baptist in Lk. 3:3; Ac. 10:37) and as its object either 'the message of the kingdom' (Lk. 8:1; 9:2; Ac. 20:25; 28:31) or Jesus Christ (Ac. 8:5; 9:20; 10:42; 19:13). The flavour of the word, while clearly controlled largely by the subject matter of Luke's two volumes, suggests the announcement of something new and previously unknown to the audience.[59] That Luke chooses this term to describe Jewish preaching in the synagogues perhaps suggests that he was thinking of the preaching to Gentiles who attended the synagogue (e.g. Jos. *Bell.* II.560; VII.45) rather than the regular reading and exposition of the law for Jews which was the main purpose of synagogue gatherings. This would confirm the view that verse 21 is to be connected with verse 20 rather than verse 19 and that it justifies the decree on the grounds that many Gentiles were already familiar with these Mosaic demands. It is still unclear, however, which demands are in mind and by no means certain that they are an adaptation of the levitical rules for 'strangers in the land', as is commonly supposed. All we can say is that the terms of the decree are in some sense Mosaic and consist of the sort of things which Jews 'preached' to Gentiles who attended the synagogue.

The clues in Luke's narrative do provide us with a few guidelines for further discussion of the terms of the decree, but they do not provide unambiguous evidence that settles the text or meaning of the decree with any certainty. They suggest that Luke viewed the decree as a set of obligations, imposed on Gentile Christians by the apostles, with some Mosaic connection, and likely to be familiar to Gentiles who had had previous contact with the synagogues. In the light of these preliminary considerations we can now take a closer look at the three main interpretations of the decree.

Leviticus 17–18

By far the most common interpretation of the decree is to see it as an adaptation of the prohibitions outlined in Lev. 17–18 which apply not only to Jews but also to Gentiles living among them – the so-called 'strangers in the land'.[60] The purpose of the prohibitions was to avoid pollution of the land such as had been caused by the misdeeds of Israel's pagan predecessors in Canaan. Likening Gentile converts to strangers in the land, the decree in effect imposes upon them those provisions of the law applicable to them after the extremist argument for the imposition of the whole law has been rejected. This division of opinion over the status of Gentile converts may well have had its counterpart in first-century Judaism, with Palestinian Jews demanding full proselytization before deeming a Gentile acceptable and diaspora Jews forgoing the requirement of circumcision in favour of a few minimal demands which summarized the law.[61] They may have differed from Christians in their definition of these minimal demands but in principle the distinction remains the same. If the identification of the terms of the decree with Lev. 17—18 is accepted, it is clear that Luke defines the relation of Gentiles to the law in a quite specific way: the law in general, including circumcision, is appropriate for Jewish-Christians alone; but the Gentiles are not free from the law insofar as they are bound by the rules which the law itself addressed to non-Jews.[62]

The advantages of this identification are clear. The Mosaic connection (15:21) is explained as is the distinction between greater and lesser obligations — for it is clear that the demands of the decree would have been much less of a burden than imposition of the whole law. Moreover, the order of the terms of the decree in 15:29; 21:25 (not in 15:20) is identical to, and the substance approximately the same as, the topics discussed in Lev. 17—18. The identification seems straightforward and has appeared so to the majority of modern scholars. Yet the more it is examined, in connection with the original or the Lucan setting of the decree, the more problematic it seems.

The observation about the order of the terms of the decree is significant, and yet it is interesting to note that in the one version which is often taken to be Luke's rewriting of the decree (15:20) this connection with Lev. 17—18 is obscured. Secondly, as we have already seen, in the context of Luke's narrative such an interpretation creates a considerable degree of tension with Peter's vision and the significance that Luke attaches to it in Ac. 10—11. To what seems to be a twofold summary of the law in terms of 'fearing God and acting righteously', (Ac. 10:35) specific and additional 'cultic' demands are now added. Thirdly, Luke presents the decree as apostolic rather than Mosaic in origin (Ac. 15:19, 28—9; 16:4) and we might suppose that, with his penchant for quoting the Old Testament to prove a point, he would have referred clearly to Lev. 17—18 if that was the connection he had wished to make. If it is thought that this is the function of 15:21, then it must be said that it is an unusually obscure way of making a point which in other connections Luke makes without equivocation.

A closer look at Lev. 17—18 and its relation to first-century Jewish practice does little to dispel the doubts raised by Luke's account of things. First, the rules outlined in Lev. 17–18 are not, as is often asserted, *the* rules for strangers in the land according to the law. Haenchen's comment is typical: 'What binds these four prohibitions together, and at the same time distinguishes them from all other "ritual" requirements of "Moses", is that they – and they alone – are given not only to Israel but also to the strangers dwelling among the Jews.'[63] The confidence of this assertion is undermined not only by the fact that the connection between $\pi\nu\iota\kappa\tau\acute{o}\varsigma$ and Lev. 17–18 is by any reckoning extremely obscure, but also by the presence of other commands of the law which also apply to 'strangers in the land'. The *ger*/$\pi\rho\sigma\acute{\eta}\lambda\nu\tau\sigma\varsigma$ is enjoined to keep the sabbath in Ex. 20:10; 23:12; Dt. 5:14, and the day of atonement in Lev. 16:29 – neither of which is mentioned in the decree. Moreover, while the flesh of naturally expired animals ($\theta\nu\eta\sigma\iota\mu\alpha\hat{\iota}\sigma\nu$) is forbidden in Lev. 17:15, according to Dt. 14:21 the same meat is forbidden to Jews but allowed to 'strangers' (though *ger* becomes $\pi\acute{\alpha}\rho\sigma\iota\kappa\sigma\varsigma$ in the LXX at this point). Thus strictly speaking the terms of the decree, understood in this manner, would have been an incomplete list of the Mosaic requirements for 'strangers in the land'. No explanation is forthcoming for this since we have virtually no evidence of how Lev. 17–18 was understood in first-century Judaism, let alone how it was harmonized with other parts of the law. Indeed what little evidence we do have confuses things further because, secondly, the LXX uses the term $\pi\rho\sigma\acute{\eta}\lambda\nu\tau\sigma\varsigma$ in Lev. 17–18 (Lev. 17:3, 10, 15; 18:26, etc.) as it does with the rulings on the sabbath and the day of atonement mentioned above. This would suggest that first-century Judaism, and in all probability Luke himself, would not have seen these demands as relevant to Gentile Christians (except those already fully proselytized before becoming Christians). The rules for and the status of proselytes set them apart from other Gentiles, including godfearers.[64] Indeed this raises a third problem in the identification of the decree with Lev. 17–18, namely that there is no evidence that first-century Judaism made Lev. 17–18 part of its demands for proselytes or godfearers. Proselytes had to undergo baptism, circumcision, and make an offering in the Temple as the sign of their full conversion, but there is no record of Lev. 17–18 playing a part in this – perhaps because Lev. 17–18 also applies to Jews, and proselytes would automatically become subject to it after conversion. For godfearers we know even less. They had a marginal status on the fringes of synagogue life and, however pious, technically they remained fully Gentile. The Noachic rules which have survived in later rabbinic sources prohibit the following: idolatry, incest/unchastity, shedding blood, profanation of God's name, robbery, injustice, and eating the flesh of a living animal.[65] It is not certain whether these provisions were devised at a time when Israel no longer had a land which could be polluted and thus represent a projection into an ideal future, or whether they contain a historical memory of pre-70 experience. In the first century they could have been adapted into rules particularly suitable for godfearers, but there is no evidence that this was done.[66] Some think the decree is an abbreviated form of the Noachic rules, omitting either what was self-evident or uncontroversial or what did not pertain to matters of cultic purity,[67] but the connection is tenuous at best. In the Noachic rules πνικτός is not found, the prohibition of blood refers to murder, and the notion of idolatry is broader than the specific ban on εἰδωλόθυτα as that is normally understood. Also, according to rabbinic writings, the *ger toshab*, the Gentile who keeps the Noachic rules but is not a proselyte, is free to eat meat that has not been ritually slaughtered.[68]

To summarize: the LXX translation of Lev. 17–18 suggests that the prohibitions were appropriate to Jews and proselytes but not to Gentiles, and the regulations which we know of which might have been applied to Gentiles are significantly different from the terms of the decree understood in a 'cultic' sense. Whether we are thinking of the original or the Lucan setting of the decree, a connection with Lev. 17–18 seems improbable. Of course, the leaders of the Jerusalem Church could have adapted the requirements of Lev. 17–18 without reference either to current Jewish practice or to the different use of them implied by the LXX. They might have depended on the Hebrew text and it could be that it was the use of προσήλυτος in the LXX which obscured the connection for later Christian writers, including Luke, but this seems more than a little improbable.

The problem of the connection between the decree and Lev. 17–18 is compounded when we examine the terminology in detail. The only term whose link with Leviticus is straightforward is αἷμα, since it could be an exact reference to Lev. 17:10f which prohibits the eating of blood. As a one-word summary of that section of Leviticus it is entirely appropriate. To use εἰδωλόθυτα to summarize Lev. 17:1–9 would, however, be curious. The passage deals with the appropriate location of sacrifices: they should be performed in front of the tabernacle and dedicated to YHWH, since any sacrifices 'outside the camp' were likely to be idolatrous, dedicated to the 'satyrs after whom they play the harlot' (17:7 LXX καὶ οὐ · θύσουσιν ἔτι τὰς θυσίας αὐτῶν τοῖς ματαίοις, οἷς αὐτοὶ ἐκπορνεύουσιν ὀπίσω αὐτῶν). The specific issue of eating εἰδωλόθυτα, while not unrelated to Lev. 17, scarcely catches the flavour of the passage. A more general term, such as εἰδωλολατρία, would have been more appropriate The same problem arises with πορνεία, since it too does not appear in the

LXX of Lev. 18:6f (interestingly enough, the only echo of this term is the verbal form in Lev. 17:7 which is connected with idolatry) nor is it the most natural term for summarizing these prohibitions. It is commonly assumed[69] that πορνεία in the decree refers strictly to marriages within the forbidden degrees outlined in Lev. 18:6f. This seems most improbable since, on the one hand, the common meaning of πορνεία – fornication, licentiousness, harlotry[70] – is far broader than the notion of consanguineous marriages (for which it is at any rate barely appropriate) and, on the other hand, Lev. 18 itself does not restrict discussion to this problem but includes adultery, homosexuality and bestiality among its themes (18:19f). Thus insofar as πορνεία is an appropriate term to recall Lev. 18:6f, and that may not be far, it is more appropriate to, and more likely to recall, the general sexual prohibitions of Lev. 18:19f than the problem of consanguineous marriages discussed in Lev. 18:6f.

We come finally to the most puzzling term of them all, πνικτός. The problem can be stated simply enough: we do not know precisely what the word means and the meanings we are inclined to give to it make little or no sense in the context of first-century Judaism or Christianity. It should be noted in the first place that there is no ostensible connection between πνικτός and Lev. 17–18, despite the common and misleading tendency to refer to Lev. 17:13f as that part of the levitical rules which 'explain' the use of πνικτός. Haenchen's comment is again typical:

> πνικτός: 'all flesh of beasts not slaughtered according to Jewish ritual' (Bauernfeind, 196). It is not superfluous to mention αἷμα as well: 'In practice the partaking of food consisting of or pre-pared with blood was so different from the eating of unritually slaughtered meat that it was certainly advisable to mention them separately' (Bauernfeind, 196f). Gen. 9:4 forbade the eating of πνικτόν, Lev. 3:17 the partaking of blood; Lev. 17:10–14 com-bined the two prohibitions.[71]

In fact the word πνικτός does not occur anywhere in the LXX and is extremely rare elsewhere. Only when it is defined in the manner above can any connection be found with the Torah, and especially with Lev. 17–18. Yet the definition has no linguistic basis and it is the direct result of reading the decree in terms of Lev. 17–18 and being forced to find some connection.[72] The terms used in Lev. 17:13f are 'animals which die of their own accord' (*nᵉbelah*; LXX θνησιμαῖον) and 'animals torn by a beast of prey' (*tᵉrephah*; LXX θηριάλωτος). In rabbinic discussions both terms take on a wider meaning, so that *nᵉbelah* came to refer to any animal not properly slaughtered and *tᵉrephah* to an animal which has or dies of a blemish.[73] There is no reason to connect πνικτός with either the LXX terminology in Lev. 17 or the rabbinic development of it – with the one possible exception of Nah. 2:13 LXX: 'The lion tore (*taraph*; LXX ἁρπάζω) enough for his whelps and strangled (*ḥanaq*; LXX ἀποπνίγω) for his lionesses. He filled his cave with prey (*tereph*; LXX θήρας) and his dens with torn flesh (*tᵉrephah*; LXX ἁρπάγης).' Here the compound verb ἀποπνίγω (and not the verbal adjective πνικτός) is used in parallel with the verbal form of *tereph* and in association with the noun from the same root. There are several reasons, however, why we cannot draw any firm conclusions about the meaning of πνικτός: the LXX uses the verb ἀποπνίγω rather than the simple form πνίγω from which πνικτός is derived; the direct equivalent of ἀποπνίγω is *ḥanaq* rather than *taraph*; and the normal translation of *tereph* in the LXX is θηριάλωτος. Perhaps all that this evidence does allow is that the connection which Bauernfeind and Haenchen find between πνικτός and 'all foods not ritually slaughtered', for which the rabbinic term is *nᵉbelah* rather than *tᵉrephah*, is distinctly improbable.

The appearance of πνικτός in the decree is puzzling enough in itself,[74] and the problems are merely compounded when we try to find a connection with Lev. 17–18. Apart from all the uses of πνικτός, or its Latin equivalents, in Christian writers dependent on Acts or some other form of the apostolic decree, there is not much evidence for the meaning of this word. Many assume that since πνικτός is derived from πνίγω, whose primary meaning is 'strangle' or 'suffocate', its basic meaning is 'strangled thing'. Though acceptable linguistically this still leaves us with the need to explain why the reference to strangling occurs and to what it refers. A rather different meaning of πνικτός is attested in Classical sources. Here it is a culinary term and refers to a particular method of cooking, though precisely what is meant is not clear. Most of the examples occur in Greek Comedies no longer extant except in fragments or in Athenaeus' *Deipnosophistae*. In IX.396*a* Athenaeus attempts to define πνικτός by quotations from a variety of authors (cf. IV.147; VII.295; X.449b) which leave us not a great deal wiser. It is usually taken to mean stewing or casseroling meat in a rich sauce, sometimes with the implication that it is a delicacy. The definitions of Galen and Hesychius are less precise but point in the same direction: Galen (VI, p. 707.1) distinguishes 'things called πνικτός' from roast (ὀπτός) or boiled (ἐφθέος) food, and Hesychius defines it as a kind of roasting or baking (ὀπτάω). It is commonly assumed that this culinary sense has no bearing on the meaning of πνικτός in the decree.[75] However, the evidence of Galen (175 C.E.) and Athenaeus (*c.* 200 C.E.), though often in quotations of much earlier material, is sufficiently close chronologically for us to bear it in mind as a possible clue to the meaning of πνικτός in Acts. It does, after all, deal with the preparation of food, which is not inappropriate to the decree as it is commonly understood.

Herzog restores πνικτός to an inscription found in the Asclepion at Kos,[76] which he dates to the first half of the third century B.C.E. Though found in an Asclepion he considers the text to be a ritual prescription for priestesses of the Demeter cult: they are to avoid various sources of contamination – impure men, hero-shrines, women in childbirth, corpses – and τῶν θνασ[ιδίων μηδὲ τῶν κενεβρείων μηδὲ τῶν πνι]κτῶν μηδενὸς ἔσθεν. As an alternative to μηδὲ τῶν κενεβρείων he considers (but rejects) μηδενὸς ἅπτεσθαι (cf. Lev. 11:39), i.e. touching the dead rather than eating the flesh of animals that had died a natural death. The restoration of πνικτός is uncertain. If correct, it is interesting that it occurs in a cultic context although not at all clear what it signified in the Demeter cult. The connection with θνασίδιον (also restored to the text) recalls the use of θνησιμαῖον in Lev. 17:14 (cf. Lev. 11:40; 22:8; Dt. 14:20). Herzog inclines towards the Classical meaning for πνικτός – a means of preparing food by 'suffocation in a closed pan' rather than 'strangled meat' with blood still in it. In the last resort this obscure use of πνικτός, if it is properly restored, does little to illuminate the use of πνικτός in the decree.

In his discussion of the food laws, and especially the prohibition of blood, Philo refers to those 'of the type of Sardanapalus who greedily extend their unrestrained and excessive luxury beyond all bounds and limits. They devise novel kinds of pleasure and prepare meat unfit for the altar (ἄθυτα) by strangling and throttling (ἄγχοντες καὶ ἀποπνίγοντες) and entomb in the carcass the blood which is the essence of the soul and should be allowed to run freely away' (*Spec. Leg.* IV.122). Immediately preceding this Philo discusses the consumption of θνησιμαίων καὶ θηριαλώτων (Lev. 17:14) by non-Jews, especially the latter when hunting. The context looks encouraging and the reference to strangling promises to shed light on the use of πνικτός in the decree. It seems, however, that IV.122 is related to the preceding discussion only insofar as it deals with the consumption of blood, because it moves on to a quite different matter: Sardanapalus was a byword for gluttony and excess. The reference to throttling and strangling, therefore, probably refers to a method of preparing gourmet dishes,[77] perhaps well-known in Alexandria (Clement of Alexandria's strictures on Alexandrian gluttony come to mind). The verbs ἄγχω and ἀποπνίγω may be synonymous and may refer to the method of killing or the method of cooking. Perhaps we should take ἄγχω to refer to the killing and ἀποπνίγω to the cooking and translate:

'they prepare things without sacrificing them (i.e. without cutting their throats — a normal enough meaning of ἄθυτος), strangling and smothering (i.e. steaming) them . . . ' A degree of uncertainty remains, but Philo may be referring both to the way things were killed and the way they were cooked (for πνίγω in this sense see Herodotus II.242; Aristophanes *Av*. 511). Whatever the precise sense, it seems that Philo is referring to a minority practice, perhaps restricted to gourmets and the like, and probably known to him locally in Alexandria — none of which sheds much light on the use of πνικτός in the decree unless, with some, we suppose πνικτός to be a gloss added in Alexandria to the so-called Alexandrian (i.e. Neutral) text.

The scant evidence for the use of πνικτός thus suggests that it might refer to a method of cooking, or a method of slaughtering. Returning to the question of the connection with Lev. 17–18, how do we explain the presence of πνικτός? If it means 'strangled' it is presumably a refinement of the prohibition of blood, referring to the blood remaining in an animal slaughtered in this fashion. That this method of slaughtering was a matter of concern for Jews can be seen in Philo's comment on the way in which all things perish either for external or internal reasons: 'similarly living creatures die of themselves through disease or through external causes, being slain, or stoned or burned or suffering the unclean death of hanging (θάνατον οὐ καθαρὸν τὸν δι' ἀγχόνης ὑπομένουσιν)' (*Aet. Mund.* 20; cf. *De Mut.* 62). A later rabbinic statement says that 'All may slaughter at all times and with all instruments except the scythe, saw, teeth and finger nails, because these merely throttle (*ḥanaq*)' (Hullin 1.2). It remains unclear why this particular refinement is mentioned together with the prohibition of blood, insofar as it has no basis in Lev. 17 and the refinements mentioned there do not appear in the decree. Does it refer to butchering practices in the Gentile world and imply that while slitting the throat was the normal method, a quick twist of the neck was common with small animals and fowl? This could be so, but there is no evidence to confirm it.

It might be noted in passing that in Athenaeus' references to πνικτός, where the meat is specified, he twice mentions a milk-fed kid (IV.147 γαλακτοτρόφου πνικτάς; X.448 πνικτὰ γαλακτοθρέμμονα) or a 'newborn' and 'tender' kid (IX.396). It is perhaps just possible that πνικτός was a rare technical term referring to the cooking of young kids who, being milk-fed, would be 'boiled in their mother's milk'. The prohibition of this in Dt. 14:21 (in connection with θνησιμαῖον), Ex. 23:19; 34:26, became the basis of an important set of rules about mixing meat and dairy products. It is discussed in Hullin 8.1f and remains an important dietary rule for Jews to this day. The problem is that the connection with the term πνικτός may be fortuitous and may reside only in the context which Athenaeus provides.

In conclusion we can note that while it is possible to explain πυκτός as an extension or refinement of the prohibition of blood, it is strange that this and this alone is considered sufficiently significant to be included in a decree regulating the behaviour of Gentile Christians. The only contemporary Jewish evidence which shows a similar concern is found in Philo and his brief allusion seems to refer to a local, or at least, minority, practice such as would hardly be the subject of legislation in the decree. It is the sheer strangeness of πυκτός which, quite as much as the textual variations, causes some to suspect that it is a local, possibly an Alexandrian, addition.[78] Moreover, the evidence we have reviewed reinforces any doubts about a direct connection between the decree and Lev. 17–18, whether it is viewed historically or in its Lucan context.

Whatever may be the precise connection, if any, with Lev. 17–18, and whether we include πυκτός or not, the decree read in one way amounts to a threefold prohibition with a basis in Mosaic laws: εἰδωλόθυτα, πορνεία and αἷμα / πυκτός. How would Luke and his readers view them? We know that Luke presents them as more apostolic than Mosaic, as inspired by the Spirit (Ac. 15:28), and we can safely assume that they were widely accepted among Gentile Christians in his day. The problem of εἰδωλόθυτα is rarely mentioned outside Christian writings (IV Macc. 5:2; Ps. Phoc. 31),[79] is discussed at some length by Paul in I Cor. 8–10, and is referred to briefly in Rev. 2, Did. 6:3 and Justin *Dial.* 34f. In his discussion with the Corinthians Paul distinguishes between eating idol-food (which was lawful but not always advisable) and eating it in the context of a pagan cult-meal (which he condemned). This distinction did not, however, survive, and by the end of the first century a Christian's attitude towards the consumption of idol-food became one of the tests of 'orthodoxy'. To eat idol-food was to 'worship dead gods' (Did. 6:3) and was characteristically practised by libertine gnostics (Just. *Dial.* 34f). Thus close to the time Luke wrote, the prohibition of εἰδωλόθυτα was no longer a food law based on Mosaic principles or responding to Jewish scruples, but an important means of distinguishing between two different kinds of Christians. Eating idol-food thus signified something much broader — participation in a pagan cult — in effect εἰδωλολατρία or, as Luke has it in Ac. 15:20, 'the pollutions of idols'.

The ban on πορνεία is a standard part of Christian exhortation and occurs throughout the New Testament (I Cor. 5–7; II Cor. 12:21; Gal. 5:19; Eph. 5:3; Col. 3:5; I Thess. 4:3; Rev. 2:21; 9:21; 14:8; 17:2, 4; 18:3; 19:2). As is often noted, many of these refer to πορνεία in connection with or in the same list as idolatry (Rev. 2:14, 20; I Cor. 5:11; 6:9; 10:6–8) and, in connection with εἰδωλόθυτα, this may be the specific allusion Luke and his readers discovered in the decree. More broadly, πορνεία was considered by Jews and Christians to be one of the hallmarks of the Gentile world and, with some exceptions, among Christians avoiding it was one of the hallmarks of true conversion.

The prohibition of blood is not mentioned in any early Christian documents, apart from the decree, until the late second century and beyond (Tertullian *Apol.* IX.13; Minucius Felix *Octav.* 30; Eusebius *Hist.* V.1.26), and then usually in connection with pagan charges of cannibalism. Tertullian, for example, argues that since Christians do not eat animal blood it is highly improbable that they would consume human blood: 'We do not even have the blood of animals at special meals. This is why we refrain from eating the meat of any animals which have been strangled or that die of themselves, lest we be in any way contaminated with blood, even if it is hidden in the flesh.' There is, however, no evidence that the charge of cannibalism in any way concerns Luke. Minucius Felix connects the two things differently, by suggesting that Christians have such an awe for human blood (i.e. life) that they do not even eat animal blood in their food. The link between eating (animal) blood and shedding (human) blood is not unprecedented, because the two themes are frequently mentioned in the same breath in the Old Testament and Jewish writings (Gen. 9:4–6; Ez. 33:25; Jub. 6:7–8; 7:28f; 21:18f), showing that it was natural to move from the one to the other. Whether in Luke's mind there was a connection between abstention from animal blood and a respect for human life must remain uncertain, though there are Jewish precedents for an easy shift from one to the other. We can at least surmise why the problem of 'blood' drops out of sight and why abstention from it would not have seemed a 'burden' in Luke's day. First, meat was not a major dietary item in the ancient world and would normally have been eaten only on special occasions (see Tertullian above). Secondly, while there is some evidence to show that not all meat on sale in ancient markets was εἰδωλόθυτα,[80] it is probable that a great deal of it was.[81] A safe route for Christians seeking to avoid idol-food was to abstain from meat altogether – a decision which, as Ehrhardt shows, could have a devastating effect on the economy.[82] At the same time this would largely resolve the problem of blood since meat was the place where blood would normally be found. In other words, abstention from αἷμα (and πνικτός?) may well have been a non-issue for many early Christians since avoiding them was a natural by-product of observing the more important prohibition of idol-food.

We can thus draw two conclusions. First, that by the time Luke wrote (*c.* 90 C.E.) it is probable that abstention from those things banned by the decree was an established part of Gentile Christian mores, and this alone largely explains why Luke can present the decree as in no substantial sense a burden and as likely to receive a warm welcome among Gentile churches.[83] It is perhaps in this sense that Luke describes the terms of the decree as ἐπάναγκες, i.e. they are obligations, but obligations of a customary rather than a legal sort, a familiar and accepted part of Christian practice which the decree merely confirms. This view of the decree might have been reinforced if non-Christian Gentiles followed some of the same rules, either because similar demands were made of godfearers or because non-Jews sometimes chose to adopt certain Jewish customs. The evidence of Philo (*Vit. Mos.* II.202f) and Josephus (*Ap.* II.282) to this effect is, allowing for some exaggeration, pertinent as is the decision of Seneca to give up vegetarianism for fear that he would be associated with 'foreign superstitions' (Judaism? Christianity? Cf. Sen. *Ep.* CVIII.22 and Juv. *Sat.* VII.161, XIV.96f). If πνικτός was banned in some pagan cults, as the evidence from Kos may show, this may have made it all the more familiar when it appeared in the decree.

Secondly, whatever the original connection between the decree and Mosaic law – and having a Mosaic connection does not necessarily imply an exclusive reference to Lev. 17–18 – it is obscured both by Luke's insistence that the decree was apostolic in origin and inspired by the Spirit and by the way in which the terms of the decree were in all probability understood at the time he wrote. What may have started life as a set of limited 'cultic' regulations had already by the turn of the century acquired a broader significance. Indeed, even when πνικτός is included, the distinction between 'cultic' and 'ethical' breaks down. For by the time Luke wrote, the understanding of the decree had in all probability passed beyond mere obedience to levitical rules of purity – moving, in fact, towards the ethical view of the Western text – and in part had gained new significance in the context of the internal dispute over libertine gnostics and, just possibly even at this early stage, the external slanders of the Roman world.

Put briefly, it is improbable that Luke and his readers would have understood the decree exclusively as a set of levitical or cultic regulations – an understanding of them which is not without its problems even when considering their historical origin.

Pagan cults

From time to time it has been suggested that the purpose of all the pro-

visions of the decree was to discourage Christians from any connection
with the idolatrous worship of pagan cults. Lake, for example, mentions it
as one viable interpretation[84] – though he omits discussion of πνικτός
which he believes to be a later addition and provides very little evidence to
justify this interpretation of the other terms of the decree. Kümmel provides the fullest defence of this view by the use of later Jewish-Christian
evidence.[85] This is one direction the argument might take, and the other is
to consider how the terms of the decree individually fit the context of
pagan worship.

There are certain advantages to this line of enquiry and it is surprising
that it has not been more actively pursued. It would fit readily with the
Cornelius narrative in Ac. 10–11, since it would be self-evident that a
Gentile convert would be required to abandon worship of other gods and
the cults associated with them, and clear that Cornelius, as a godfearer,
would already have done this. Pertinent, too, is the observation that the
two main speeches addressed to Gentiles (Ac. 14:15f; 17:22f) concern
themselves above all with the contrast between the vain, idolatrous worship of pagan gods and worship of the one true God. Luke thus indicates
that idolatry was the hallmark of a Gentile and the main feature of his life
which would have to change. This view is deeply rooted in the Old Testament and Jewish literature, and its prominence in hellenistic Jewish
apologetic writings provides a particularly convincing explanation for the
reference to the 'preaching' of Moses in Ac. 15:21. If there was one thing
above all which could be said to control the Jewish view of the Gentiles
and the appeals they made to them, it was the conviction that they were
idolaters;[86] and not only was idolatry believed to be their main short-
coming, it was also held to be the basis of all other forms of Gentile
immorality (Wisd. 12–14; Jub. 2:16–18; Sib. Or. 4:28–32).

That the decree may have been interpreted in this fashion is indicated
by the condemnation in Revelation of those who teach Christians φαγεῖν
εἰδωλόθυτα καὶ πορνεῦσαι (Rev. 2:14, slightly different in 2:20) and the
promise οὐ βάλλω ἐφ᾽ ὑμᾶς ἄλλο βάρος (Rev. 2:24), which may well echo
Ac. 15:28. It would appear that in both Pergamum and Thyatira Christians
were persuaded by gnostic libertines (Nicolaitans) to participate in pagan
worship – πορνεύω – referring either literally to the sexual activities of
these cults or metaphorically to idolatry as a form of harlotry (see below).
That 'blood' is not mentioned may be because it was not a matter of controversy or because it was effectively subsumed under 'idol-food'. It may
be that the author of Revelation is deliberately recalling these communities
to the terms of the apostolic decree as the norm for regulating Gentile
Christian practice and, even if not, these references show that there is no

difficulty in supposing that the decree was in force in Asia Minor around the turn of the century — the same time and place which many ascribe to the author of Acts.[87] Of all the evidence which has a bearing on the meaning of the decree this is closest in time to the date of the composition of Acts and, while the precise relation with the decree remains unclear and the place of composition of Acts even more so, at the least it shows how some terms of the decree could have been understood at the time Luke wrote and that this understanding might not have been intended by those who originally devised the decree.

Initially, then, the association of all terms of the decree with the problem of idolatry and pagan worship is an attractive explanation of Luke's understanding of it. Kümmel seeks confirmation in later Christian literature, especially the Pseudo-Clementines.[88] The two most important passages prohibit participation in the 'table of demons', which they define as follows: 'λέγω δὲ εἰδωλοθύτων νεκρῶν πνικτῶν θηριαλώτων αἵματος' (Hom. VII.8.1); 'hoc est, immolata degustare vel sanguinem vel morticinium quod est suffocatum, et si quid illud est quod daemonibus oblatum est' (Rec. IV.36.4). In both passages participation in pagan sacrificial meals is linked to and defined by (λέγω δέ, hoc est) a list of things which include three of the terms of the decree, including the troublesome πνικτός.[89] It seems from Hom. VIII.19.1 that the connection between the lists and the 'tables of demons' rests upon the distinctive demonology of the Pseudo-Clementines. It is generally agreed that the decree has at some stage influenced these writings, perhaps when the *Grundschrift* was composed around 200 C.E.,[90] or perhaps at a later date when the problems of the 'tables of demons' and the 'tables of the Gentiles' were fused.[91] The essential question for our purposes is whether this evidence provides a clue to the original, or at least the Lucan, meaning of the decree. The important terms are αἷμα and πνικτός since the connection of εἰδωλόθυτα and πορνεία with pagan cults can be demonstrated on other grounds. It is important to note that the evidence cannot be dismissed as a Gentile Christian misunderstanding of originally Jewish issues since, whenever we date it, it is evidence of a Jewish-Christian understanding of the decree. Its value would be enhanced if we could assume that it reflected a common understanding of the decree in Jewish-Christian circles during the second century, but of this we cannot be sure.[92]

A similar way of explaining αἷμα and πνικτός is found in Origen's statement:

> 'For that which is offered to idols is sacrificed to demons and a man of god must not join in the table of demons. As to things

strangled, we are forbidden by Scripture to partake of them
because the blood is still in them; and blood, especially the odour
arising from the blood, is said to be the food of demons. Perhaps
then, if we were to eat strangled animals, we might have such
spirits feeding along with us. And the reason which forbids the
use of strangled animals is also applicable to the use of blood'
(*Contra Celsum* 8.30).

The notion of demons eating the blood of sacrifices has ancient roots in
chthonic cults of various kinds (cf. Homer *Od.* 11) and is found elsewhere
in Christian writers (Tertullian *Apol.* XXII.6; Athenagoras *Leg.* 27;
Clement of Alexandria *Paed.* XI.1—8) and the identification of pagan
deities with demons is a commonplace Jewish and Christian theme (Dt.
32:17; Is. 55:11 LXX; I En. 19:1; 99:7; Jub. 1:11; I Cor. 10; Just. *Apol.*
I.5). Origen's explanation of $αἷμα/πνικτός$ is consistent with that found in
the Pseudo-Clementines and shows that the terms of the decree could be
associated with pagan worship in both Gentile and Jewish Christian circles.
This evidence still has to be used with some caution since Origen's view, at
least, could well be an attempt to explain a regulation whose original
intention had been forgotten. On the other hand, the allusions in Revelation could be said to provide us with a link which takes us back to the
time of Luke and shows that the view of the Pseudo-Clementines and
Origen, far from being a late second-century innovation, may represent a
long-established (even if mistaken) view of the meaning of the decree.

A somewhat different tack is to consider the terms of the decree in the
broader context of pagan cultic practices. In this context the term
$εἰδωλόθυτα$ is, of course, straightforward and requires no further comment, and $πορνεία$ fits well in a literal or a metaphorical sense. Taken literally it would refer to the various forms of sexual activity (especially sacred
prostitution) associated with a number of pagan cults.[93] As a metaphor for
participation in idolatrous worship it has a long history in Jewish and
Christian traditions (e.g. Mic. 1:7; Jer. 3:1—9; Is. 57:9; Wisd. 14:2; Rev.
2:14, 20) and there is no difficulty in understanding the term in this way
in the decree, especially in conjunction with $εἰδωλόθυτα$.

That $αἷμα$ refers to the bloody rites of pagan sacrifices, one of their
most prominent features, is certainly feasible. Already in Jewish traditions
their own bloody sacrificial rites are singled out for criticism (Prov. 21:3;
Is. 1:11; Ps. 50:13) and the Sibylline Oracles (4:29—30) speak of pagan
altars that are 'befouled with the constant blood of living things and quad-
rupeds'. Apart from this general association, more specific allusions could
be in mind — for example the rite of Taurobolium in the Mithras cult, or

the blood rites associated with cult officials attached to oracle centres (Paus. II.24.1; III.16.9). It was also the custom in some cults to drink the blood of the victim, often mingled with wine, as part of the sacred meal (Plato *Critias* 120A; cf. Is. 65:4; 66:3, 17), although it is not clear that this practice persisted into the Roman period. Insofar as such rites even suggested the consumption of blood it would make them abhorrent to a Jew. Another possible association of 'blood' could be the bloody flesh of the victims which as a rule was either consumed by the devotees on the temple premises, taken home for later use, or sold in the market. Jews would abhor it both because it contained blood and because it had been used in idolatrous rites. It is not difficult, therefore, to see how blood could have been associated in a variety of ways with pagan cults, especially if that association had already been established by other terms of the decree.

The term ποικτός is, as always, more troublesome. If we take it to mean 'strangled things' it is not clear to what it may refer.[94] The normal method of sacrifice in the ancient world involved a release of blood by cutting the victim's neck, though animals were sometimes stoned (Eurip. *Androm.* 1128; Paus. II.32) or clubbed (Apollonius Rhodius *Argon.* I.426; Dionysius Halicarnassensis VII.72:15). Although strangling was the normal method in India and known to be so by the Classical world (Strabo XV.1.54) there is no evidence that this custom travelled westwards and had any influence on Graeco-Roman practice.[95] The Scythians were known to throttle their sacrificial beasts with a kind of tourniquet (Herodotus IV.60), but Herodotus describes it as a curiosity. Most of what we know about cultic practice concerns the large and public festivals and we have few insights into the operation of local shrines. One might wonder whether in the regular round of votive offerings, involving for the average citizen a modest hen or other small animal (Paus. X.32.16), throttling might have been more common than in the great festivals. Herodas (*Mimes* IV) describes the visit to a local Asclepium by two garrulous women. The priest sacrifices the hen in a back room, takes his portion, and the rest is taken home by the women, but we are not told how the bird was killed.[96] All in all this route does not take us far. If we consider the other possible sense of πνικτός — something steamed or cooked — we do not get much further. Long ago Schneckenburger suggested that it was a reference to Roman epicures who ate fowls suffocated in Falernian wine.[97] Perhaps a more plausible allusion would be to the widespread custom of cooking the innards of sacrificial beasts, offering selected portions to the deity, and sharing the rest among the worshippers.[98] Plautus (*Rud.* 135) mentions how someone living close to a temple complained of the constant borrowing of articles for use in the rites, including a 'pot to cook the guts in' (cf. Varro *Ling. Lat.* V.98; Suet. *Aug.* 1). This appears to have been a frequent practice in a number of cults, but there is no evidence that πνικτός was used to describe it. In the light of the available evidence the more plausible way to connect πνικτός with pagan cults is in the manner of the Pseudo-Clementines and Origen, although the term itself is so obscure that a reference to some other aspect of pagan worship cannot be excluded. Alternatively, if for other reasons this understanding of the decree is thought to be persuasive as far as Luke is concerned, we might suppose that πνικτός was a later, local addition for reasons now unknown.

In the context of Luke's narrative this interpretation makes a great deal of sense. It is true that although the general question of Gentile idolatry is addressed in Ac. 14 and 17 the more specific issue of participation in pagan cults is not a live issue in Acts, but this may be because the decree was in force in the Lucan communities and not a matter of controversy. Otherwise it fits the flow of Luke's narrative, makes sense of Ac. 15:21, and accords with an understanding of the decree which we can with some plausibility trace from approximately the same time (and maybe the same place) that Luke wrote to Jewish and Gentile Christian circles in the second and third centuries. The awkward term is, as before, πνικτός, and we would have to suppose that Luke understood it in one of the ways suggested above or that it was not in his text.

Ethical rules

A fully ethical interpretation of the decree requires the omission of πνικτός. It is easier to make a case for this with respect to the Lucan than with respect to the original form of the decree, but the matter remains uncertain. That 'strangling' could be raised in connection with the prohibition of blood and in an ethical sense is shown by the rabbinic comment (Gen. R. on 34:14) that 'the one who strangles' is still to be considered 'a shedder of human blood'. But for such a meaning to be implied by the decree would require a different form from the verbal adjective πνικτός.

That the decree could be understood in an ethical way is of course shown by the Western texts, and it is a view which has a great deal in its favour besides. The Noachic rules and the Sibylline Oracles, for example, appeal to the Gentiles in much the same way, and there is evidence to show that the Jews viewed the three cardinal sins of the Gentiles to be precisely those of idolatry, shedding of blood and sexual immorality. Indeed it is these three categories which Strack and Billerbeck use to categorize the evidence they collect in connection with the Jewish view of the non-Jewish world.[99] This in turn recalls those rabbinic passages, often assigned to the time of Hadrian, in which Jews are advised that under extreme duress Mosaic laws could be ignored with the exception of the prohibition of idolatry, immorality and murder (Seb. 7*b*; Sanh. 24*a*). Moreover, this interpretation would make excellent sense of Acts 15:21, since we have evidence to show that diaspora Jews frequently summarized the law into a few basic demands and Philo (*Spec. Leg.* II.62f) seems to imply that they presented it in this form to interested Gentiles who attended the synagogue. Luke, too, reveals an interest in precisely such summaries of the law in his Gospel (Lk. 10:25f; 11:41) and such an interpretation would, of course, accord best of all with the Cornelius narrative in general and Peter's summary of its significance (Ac. 10:35) in particular.

This interpretation requires that εἰδωλόθυτα be taken as more or less equivalent to εἰδωλολατρία. This perhaps receives some support from the paraphrase 'pollutions of idols' in Ac. 15:20 and, as we have seen, in a different context among later Christian writers abstention from idol-food is understood broadly as a symbol of orthodoxy. The term πορνεία would presumably refer to fornication in particular but also to sexual licentiousness in general, both of which meanings are common enough elsewhere. The essential difference between this view of the decree and the first option discussed above, viewed from a Lucan point of view, would be that 'blood' would be taken as a prohibition of murder. The absolute use of 'blood' with no accompanying verb is rare, but it is clear that in the Old Testament and Jewish writings it means both the consumption of blood (usually with ἐσθίω in LXX) and the shedding of blood (usually with ἐκχέω in LXX). The latter meaning is much the more frequent and it is clear that the shedding of blood was believed to cause pollution just as much as its consumption (Judith 8:21; Is. 59:3; Lam. 4:13–14; and Ez. 22:4, which connects the 'pollution of idols' with the 'shedding of blood'). Frequently, too, the two notions of shedding and eating blood are mentioned together as if they are two sides of the same coin (Gen. 9:4–6; Ez. 33:25; Jub. 6:7–8; 7:28f). For what it is worth it might also be noted that 'blood' is the only term of the decree used elsewhere in Luke–Acts, where it always means 'kill' or 'murder' and never refers to the eating of blood (Lk. 11:50–5; 13:1; Ac. 5:28; 22:20). This may indicate Luke's understanding of 'blood' in the decree but, since he may be quoting official or traditional versions of it, the terminology of the decree cannot so easily be controlled by Luke's usage elsewhere.

To put it briefly, an 'ethical' understanding of the decree is the one which fits most smoothly into the immediate context in Acts (ch. 10–15), agrees with the view of the law which Luke expresses elsewhere, and can be shown to have interesting parallels in both diaspora and Palestinian Jewish contexts which make good sense of Ac. 15:21. Against this one must set the necessity of omitting πνικτός and the view that the very coherence of this interpretation may be precisely why an original πνικτός was quietly dropped from the text.

Summary

A lengthy discussion of the decree has been required not only because it is difficult to understand and has attracted an immense body of scholarship and because of its centrality to Luke's view of Gentile obligation to the law, but also because of the need to review the evidence while keeping in mind a clear distinction between the original and the Lucan understanding of the decree. With respect to the text it was noted that many of the arguments appropriate to a discussion of the original form of the decree are less relevant and persuasive when considering its Lucan form. The consequence is not that the Western text, or something close to it, can confidently be accepted, but merely that it is reinstated as a credible option in Luke's account. If πνικτός is omitted the 'ethical' interpretation unquestionably fits best into Luke's narrative, with a reference to pagan worship running a close second. If πνικτός is included the 'ethical' interpretation is ruled out and one of the other two interpretations must be assumed, although in either case πνικτός remains the awkward term to explain. Whatever the original purpose of the terms of the decree, and however precisely Luke understood them, it seems unlikely that he or his readers would have understood them as an adaptation of Lev. 17–18. Even if originally they had a 'cultic' sense, by Luke's time they were an accepted part of Christian mores, with an apostolic rather than a Mosaic imprimatur, and adherence to at least some of them had taken on a quite different motivation. Essentially they were a set of ecclesiastical provisions. A basis for them could be found in Mosaic law, as was true of much earlier Gentile Christian practice and belief, but they were not seen as the imposition of Mosaic law as such. They were to be kept not because they were Mosaic but because they were apostolic. That is, accepting the terms of the decree, as for example accepting an obligation to keep the double love command which Luke refers to elsewhere, would for Gentile Christians in part be based on their appearance in scripture but, more important, on their appearance in the teaching of Jesus and the apostles. In neither case would they be seen as the imposition of Jewish law.

A number of conclusions can thus be drawn from the evidence of Acts.

It is made unquestionably clear that living according to the law ultimately has no bearing on the salvation of Jews or Gentiles. At the same time it is always implicit, and on one occasion explicit (Ac. 21), that there is no conflict for Jews between living according to the law, indeed doing so zealously, and being a Christian. As a means of expressing piety, as distinct from a means of achieving salvation, it is viewed in a wholly positive light. Both the manner and the degree to which this aspect of the law is dominated by the figure of Paul suggest that, in addition to his approval of life according to the law for Jewish Christians in general, Luke was concerned about Paul's reputation for faithfulness to the law in particular. The relation of Gentile Christians to the law is less clear. In Ac. 10:35 the summary of behaviour appropriate for those wishing to gain salvation recalls similar summaries of the law in hellenistic Judaism and in Luke's Gospel, and the decree, however understood, has some connection with the teaching of Moses. In both instances, however, Luke makes it clear that it is the apostolic rather than the Mosaic inspiration of such teaching which is important, and that the type of obedience to the law which is appropriate for Jews is not appropriate for Gentiles. That Gentiles should not be circumcised nor keep all the laws of Moses is clear, but precisely where this leaves them with respect to Mosaic law is not. It seems unlikely, however, that Luke saw the decree as a summary of Lev. 17–18 which was to be enforced in order to fulfil the requirements which the law itself made of non-Jews. Even if this was its original meaning, and there is some doubt about that, in the circumstances of Luke's day it had a quite different significance.

It is perhaps worth repeating, as we noted with respect to the Gospel, that the law understood as prophecy plays an important role in Acts even though there are no programmatic statements quite like those found in Lk. 24 (cf. Ac. 13:22–43). A number of specific events are thus explained – for example the defection of Judas (Ac. 1:20) and Pentecost (Ac. 2:17–21) – but the main themes are the incarnation, death, resurrection and exaltation of Jesus (Ac. 2:35–8, 34–5; 3:18; 8:22–3; 13:34–5; 17:2–3), the rejection of Jesus by the Jews and the acceptance of him by Gentiles (Ac. 3:25; 4:25; 10:43; 13:41, 47; 15:16–18; 28:26–8). No more in Acts than in the Gospel is there any attempt to bring this feature into line with other discussions of the law.

4 LAW, JUDAISM AND THE GENTILES

In this chapter an attempt will be made to draw together the threads of the preceding argument and reflect upon their consequences. In particular, when we have described the various strains in Luke's narrative, we shall consider why they are so and how his view of this particular aspect of Judaism concurs with his view of Judaism and the Jews as a whole.

(1) An important motif in Luke's view of the law is that it is the *ethos* of a particular *ethnos*. As such it is akin to the views of hellenistic Jews and cultured pagans both of whom, though for different reasons, describe Jewish laws as 'customs'. It represents an enlightened, tolerant and, in Jewish writers, apologetic approach to the distinctive way of life of the Jews, in which their laws/customs are viewed as the natural and legitimate expression of their nationhood. The connection with hellenistic Judaism is the more interesting and is reinforced by Luke's interest in summaries of the law into a few basic (often ethical) commands which, it appears, he considered to be incumbent upon all Christians regardless of their origin (Lk. 10:25f; 11:41; Ac. 10:35; 15:20–1). Precisely the same tendency to summarize the law into a few basic commands marks many diaspora Jewish writings, especially when they appeal to the non-Jewish world. A connection with hellenistic Jewish views has frequently and convincingly been noted in the speech of Stephen, and O'Neill has suggested that the description of heroic figures, the appeal to the state and the theology of conversion are features of Acts which belong to the same world of thought.[1] Moreover, the speech to the Gentiles ascribed to Paul in Ac. 17 also has significant points of contact with hellenistic Jewish apologetic writings.[2] Indeed this speech, together with Ac. 14:15–17, provides an interesting complement to Luke's view of Jewish legal piety, since here Gentile piety is also viewed with a certain magnanimity and optimism, as something which provides a useful preparation for the gospel, even though it is corrected and supplemented by it.[3] It is perhaps worth noting in passing that Luke does not attempt to blend his understanding of Jewish law with the concept of law in popular philosophical thought in the manner of

some hellenistic Jewish writers — a procedure which Paul, for example, echoes in Rom. 2.

Luke's view of the law is thus one aspect of his writings which, like several others, is illuminated when seen against the background of hellenistic Jewish thought. We cannot, of course, assume direct influence since the hellenistic Jewish elements may well have come down to Luke through a Christian tradition which had already appropriated them, but whether direct or indirect the connection remains. The most important consequence for Luke's view of the law is that the laws/customs of Moses are viewed as the proper and peculiar possession of the Jews, appropriate to the expression of Jewish and Jewish-Christian piety but out of place if imposed upon Gentiles.

Insofar as Luke provides a theoretical or theological underpinning for this notion it is to be found in the conviction that God is 'impartial' (οὐ προσωπολήπτης Ac. 10:34) and 'makes no distinction' (οὐθὲν διέκρινεν Ac. 15:9) between Jews and Gentiles. What God reveals of his own attitude in the Cornelius story presumably expresses the view which Luke himself held and which he believed to be appropriate for all Christians. Jews are to be accepted as Jews, and Gentiles as Gentiles. The piety of the one is as good as the piety of the other and it would be both pointless and inappropriate to expect the one to live like the other. Both rely for salvation exclusively upon Christ (Ac. 4:12), a salvation which rests upon faith and grace (Ac. 15:11), and being a Jew or a Gentile brings no advantage since both can be valuable preparation for reception of the gospel.

The conviction that God does not discriminate between Jews and Gentiles[4] and that the law contains the ἔθος of the Jewish ἔθνος I would take to be fundamental to Luke's understanding of the law and not, as Jervell contends, the belief that because the Church is the renewed or true Israel it is committed — Jew and Gentile alike — to the law as a sign of its own identity, so that 'Luke's view of the law is bound up with his ecclesiology.'[5] Jervell's discussion of the law in Luke—Acts, unquestionably the most interesting available, draws upon several other essays on related themes and it would be inappropriate to review them all here.[6] With respect to his discussion of the law it is sufficient to note that neither his assessment of Jesus' attitude towards the law in Luke's Gospel nor his view that the apostolic decree summarizes the demands of the law applicable to Gentiles — both of which are crucial to his overall thesis that both Jewish and Gentile Christians are in every respect obedient to the law — can be convincingly maintained. And if it is true, as seems to be the case, that Luke viewed the Church as the inheritor of the promises to Israel, as the true or renewed Israel, there is no evidence that he considered Gentile participation to depend upon a successful renewal of the old Israel or that the Church was thereby obliged to keep the law in all respects. Luke's view of the law and his view of the Church and Israel are developed in different ways and for different reasons and, as far as I can see, the one has nothing much to do with the other.

(2) The consequences of this view of the law for Jewish and Gentile Christians can be further spelled out. For Jewish Christians, living according to the law, even doing so zealously (Ac. 21), was a legitimate and useful expression of their piety and a natural expression of their Jewishness. Even though zeal for the law could not bring salvation, there is no doubt that Luke saw nothing incompatible between such zeal and being a Christian. This is already implicit in the birth narratives (Lk. 1—2), in Jesus' emphasis upon doing the law (Lk. 10:25f) and certain hints about his own practice in this regard, in the stories about the early Christian leaders in Acts and most especially in the firm defence of Stephen and Paul against the charge that they had undermined the authority of the law.

This is perhaps the dominant impression a Christian reader would receive, but the pattern does not remain unbroken. In the Gospel stories Jesus' teaching on divorce and the sabbath runs counter to current Jewish practice and law and it would be natural for Christian readers to understand them to imply the subjection of the law to the teaching of Jesus, a subjection which could also lead to an alteration of the law. In neither case does Luke draw attention to the legal consequences of Jesus' teaching and the stories and sayings which present a somewhat different view of the law to some extent neutralize the implicit critique. In general, Acts is more consistent than the Gospel in its attitude towards Jewish and Jewish-Christian commitment to the law, but if Luke did understand Peter's vision in Ac. 10 to involve the abolition of at least one aspect of Jewish law then even Acts is not wholly unambivalent on this matter. The simplest way to explain this is to suppose that while in general Luke approved of Jewish-Christian adherence to the law, this was an issue of no immediate concern to him or to the communities for whom he wrote. There is good reason to suppose that at the time Acts was written active missionary work among the Jews had ceased[7] although, as the evidence of Justin's *Dialogue* 47 shows, Jewish-Christians continued to exist and were in contact with Gentile Christians. Yet it seems unlikely that Jewish-Christians were even a significant minority in Luke's communities.[8] It is far easier to explain Jesus' ambivalence over the law in the Gospel and Peter's abrogation of the law in Acts if we suppose that Luke was writing for Gentiles. The former would not have been a pressing matter among Gentile Christians left to their own devices and the latter would have caused no alarm. On the other hand, if these Gentile Christians were of a Pauline stripe and Paul's reputation was under fire, it would be natural in defending him for Luke to present a consistent and exaggerated portrait of his commitment to the law.

The consequences of Luke's view for Gentile Christians are less clear, although the broad outlines can be sketched. Luke undoubtedly believed that Gentile Christians were, by and large, freed from obligation to the law by an apostolic decision approved by all the major Jewish Christian leaders. Conzelmann is thus partly right when he sees the apostolic council as the watershed which marks the Church's release from obligation to the law. This would appear to be so for Gentile Christians but not for Jewish Christians who, if not obliged to keep the law, might nevertheless, according to Lucan principles, continue to do so. Even if he is not directly addressing them, it is unlikely that Luke was unaware of the existence of Jewish-Christian believers; indeed, as we shall see, if one of his aims was to counter Jewish-Christian antagonists of Paul, he may have been only too painfully aware of them.

The Gentiles are free from the law or 'customs of Moses' because they are not their customs but the customs of the Jews. Gentiles have their own religious and cultural roots which, like those of the Jews, can be taken up in and fulfilled by the gospel of Christ. Apart from this general principle which flows from Luke's perception of the nature of Jewish law, a number of arguments are used in Acts 15 to defend the position of Gentile Christians. The decisions taken at the council were, of course, apostolic and could be shown to have a basis in scriptural prophecies – and neither of these are insubstantial observations – but the fundamental justification seems to be that God does not discriminate against those who live without the law and that they, like the Jews, will be saved on the basis of faith and grace. It is perhaps worth noting that, although he may get to it by a somewhat different route and express it in somewhat different language, Luke's overall assessment of the status of Jews and Gentiles *vis-à-vis* the law turns out to be much like the view expressed by Paul in I Cor. 7:20 that 'everyone should remain in the state in which he was called'.

Yet this is not all Luke has to say about the Gentiles and the law. Luke 10:25f; Acts 10:35; 15:20–1 imply that even among the Gentiles there should be some commitment to Mosaic principles even though there is no commitment to the law in the stricter and fuller sense. It might seem tempting to make this distinction by contrasting the 'ritual' and 'ethical' aspects of the law, but it is a distinction which Luke does not use and it all too easily leads to the view that Christians were solely interested in the ethical, and Jews in the ritual, aspects of the law. It is true that Lk. 10:25f

represents the teaching of Jesus as well as the teaching of the law and that
Ac. 10:35; 15:20–1 have an apostolic imprimatur, and it may well be that
this is how Luke resolved the tension between the view that the Gentiles
were freed from the law (with respect to such things as circumcision,
sabbath observance, food laws, etc.) and yet at the same time obligated to
its central commands ('to love God and one's neighbour', or 'to fear God
and work righteousness'). It may be that he believed that certain fundamental beliefs and moral commitments of Judaism, because they had been
affirmed by Jesus or the apostles, had become fundamental for Christians
too. The problem was by no means unique to Luke, but rather was characteristic of all forms of Christianity where the Old Testament was appropriated as scripture, mined for proof texts, and seen to provide a basis for
certain beliefs (monotheism) and practices (e.g. love of neighbour), while
at the same time many of the commands of Torah which became the basis
of Jewish praxis were simply ignored. This selective use of the Old Testament created problems from the time of Paul on, but neither he, who
worried at it more than any other, nor most other early Christian writers
found a happy solution. The issue is raised most sharply in Justin's
Dialogue (9–31) when Trypho accuses Christians of inconsistency in their
use of the Old Testament as scripture. The author of Barnabas proposes
one solution by accepting the ethical teaching of the Old Testament (in
the form of the two-ways, chs. 18f) and allegorizing all the rest (chs.
1–17), and the author of Hebrews works with typology along much the
same lines. Luke, however, hardly seems aware of the problem let alone in
a position to offer a solution.

It is hard to tell from Luke's narrative whether the question of the
Gentiles and the law was still a live issue at the time Acts was written. We
cannot doubt that Ac. 10 and 15 are pivotal passages in Luke's story and
that he considered them to have momentous significance. Yet after the
vision of Peter the question of Gentiles and the law is raised only by an
extremist Jewish Christian minority and their proposal is not only rejected
by all the significant Jerusalem leaders but, as Luke tells it, the extremists
also concur in the final decision (Ac. 15:25). After Ac. 15 the question
does not arise again and insofar as the law is a problem it is in connection
with suspicion of Paul among Jewish Christians and hostility towards him
among the 'Jews'. Thus for Luke the apostolic decision in Ac. 15 is decisive
and its authority is not challenged from that point on. The problem of the
Gentiles and the law has been solved once and for all. This may indicate
that at the time of writing the same conditions held and that the earlier
decision had established a norm for Gentile Christian practice. Insofar as
the issue may have been revived it may only have been in the sense that

Luke's readers were Pauline Christians and thus to a certain extent subject to the same slanders that were directed at their founder, but it is he rather than they who seems to concern Luke most.

(3) Jervell argues both that the real problem for Luke with respect to the law is Paul and that the attitude towards the law he ascribes to Paul is consistent with the view expressed throughout the two-volume work.[9] The first point can be confirmed by a number of observations, but the second is altogether more doubtful. The frequency with which legal terminology is associated with Paul as compared with any other figure in Acts, the monotonous accusations by his Jewish opponents that he is an enemy of the law, and the consistency of Luke's description of his faithfulness to the law are all indications that for Luke the problem of the law is primarily associated with the figure of Paul. In fact the dominance of Paul and the anxiety and defensiveness of Luke's exoneration of him suggest that it is no exaggeration to claim that for Luke the problem of the law is the problem of Paul. Or, to put it another way, it is Paul and his reputation which are crucial and the question of the law is secondary to and illustrative of this primary concern. This view of the association of the problem of the law with the problem of Paul is confirmed by Luke's apparent unconcern about the criticism of the law which he attributes to Jesus in the Gospel and perhaps in Acts 10 to Peter too. In addition to his blunt denials of Paul's antinomianism Luke calls as character-witnesses the Romans, who consistently declare Paul to be innocent, the Pharisees who agree that the dispute is over resurrection and not law,[10] and James, the one Jewish-Christian whose reputation for faithfulness to the law remained unsullied among Christian and non-Christian Jews alike.[11]

We have more than enough evidence to show that both before and after his death Paul was misunderstood by both friend and foe, and this will scarcely surprise anyone who knows from his epistles the subtle, and often barely consistent, arguments which he employed. Both his defenders (e.g. the author of Pastorals) and his detractors (e.g. the author of James) misunderstood not only because they had difficulty in understanding what he wrote — they probably had limited access to his epistles — but because the Paul they praised or decried was a mixture of fact and fantasy, rumour and cliché. The Paulinists often dulled the sharp edges and blurred the fine distinctions when transmitting the image of their hero, while his opponents often shadow-boxed with a Paul whose antinomian and anti-Jewish reputation bore little resemblance to the real man. Thus the defamers of Paul's reputation who provoked Luke's reply may well have been reacting to an image which bore no more relation to historical reality than did the image with which Luke counters them. Even among the friends of Paul there was an astonishing variety of perceptions, which encompassed gnostics (notably Valentinians) who claimed an affinity with Paul and considered his writings to be authoritative, Gentile Christian Judaizers who increasingly found Judaism and its ways attractive (Ignatius *Philad.* 6:1; cf. also Rev. 2), and thinkers such as Marcion who believed that Paul had been consistently anti-Jewish. Common to all of these, however much they may have misunderstood him, was a positive view of Paul, and none of them appears to have been the source of Luke's problem in Acts. Here the problem seems rather to be a group hostile to Paul who accuse him of being an enemy of the law.

The obvious candidates are thus Christian,[12] or non-Christian Jews,[13] and it is not too easy to decide between them. To begin with there are many problems in attempting to reconstruct the circumstances of any author from his literary products, problems which are compounded when the text is ostensibly a narrative about the past. Moreover, even if we assume that Luke is first and foremost addressing Gentile Christian readers, we cannot exclude the possibility that he had one eye cocked in the direction of their opponents. We have precious little evidence for the reaction of non-Christian Jews to Christianity in general let alone to Paul in particular. There have been attempts to discover an anti-Pauline strain in rabbinic literature, but insofar as these voluminous writings provide a recognizable anti-Christian strain at all it is directed against a distorted image of Jesus rather than against Paul. In favour of the view that the defamers of Paul were non-Christian Jews is the manner in which they consistently function as such in the narrative of Acts. If this represents the situation at the time of writing then we must assume that Luke was addressing his Christian readers exclusively, since there is little that is irenic or appealing for such Jews in the portrait of their predecessors as the malicious opponents of Paul and indeed of all other early Christian leaders.

The evidence for an anti-Pauline strain among Jewish-Christians is much more extensive and is of particular interest because their antipathy invariably centres on his alleged antinomianism. A hallmark of Jewish-Christian writings is their elevation of James and denigration of Paul. The rejection of Paul is recorded by Irenaeus (*Adv. Haer.* I.26.2; III.15.1), Origen (*c. Cels.* V.65), Eusebius (III.25.4) and Epiphanius (*Haer.* XXXVIII.5) and we are given a more specific idea of what this involved in the Pseudo-Clementines (*Rec.* I.70–3; III.49; IV.34f; *Hom.* IX.35, XVII.19f). The *Epistula Petri* 2:3–5 sets up the contrast, which is everywhere else implied, in terms of the lawfulness of Peter's teaching, his commitment to the eternal value of the law as confirmed by Jesus (Matt. 5:18), and 'the lawless and absurd doctrine of the man who is my enemy'. When we move from these statements back to an earlier period the evidence becomes more difficult to track down. Hegesippus appears in general to have ignored Paul's writings and on one occasion deliberately contradicts a statement found in I Cor. 2:9,[14] but he is apparently motivated by gnostic misuse of Paul rather than Pauline antinomianism. Among the Jewish and Jewish-Christian groups mentioned in Justin's *Dialogue* 47, one is defined as those who live according to the law and maintain that all Christians, including the Gentiles, should do so too. This directly opposes Paul's position and is akin to the view of the Judaizers he tangled with before 70 C.E. and in this sense might be considered anti-Pauline. Yet Justin may be describing a hypothetical situation and, even if he is not, we cannot assume that in defining its own position a Jewish-Christian group necessarily and deliberately opposed a Pauline, or indeed any other, view. Matt. 5:19 has occasionally been seen as an attack on Paul as the one who alters the commandments of God, and the epistle of James certainly has that ring to it too. Not only does it appear under the pseudonym of James and judge Christian behaviour in terms of obedience to the law (2:8f), but there are specific anti-Pauline echoes in the discussion of faith and works (2:14f) — and if we assume that the author is countering the view opposite to the one he propounds, then the Paulinism he refutes is already a distortion of the teaching of Paul. There is thus a fair amount of evidence, ranging from Paul's own writings before 70 C.E. to early Christian writers of the third century and beyond, that many Jewish-Christians were hostile towards Paul and that their hostility was caused above all by Paul's reputation as an antinomian. The rumour recorded in Ac. 21:21 that Paul 'teaches all the Jews who are among the Gentiles to forsake Moses, telling them not to circumcise their children or observe the customs' may well be an accurate summary of a widespread perception of Paul in Jewish-Christian circles. It could find some basis in his more extreme statements about the law, especially when these came down in garbled form and with no context, as well as in his own behaviour (I Cor. 9; Gal. 2:11f). Yet essentially it is a false perception, as Luke rightly and somewhat lopsidedly shows, in that there is no evidence to show that Paul recommended in general that Jewish-Christians should abandon their law. If it is the accusations of Jewish-Christians which spurred Luke on, his response not only rebuts them and sets the record straight but may also be said to be more irenic than it would have been if the accusers were non-Christian Jews. That is, Paul's faithfulness to the law is confirmed both by his own behaviour and by the testimony of the leading Jewish-Christians of his day, and the charges against him spring solely from the malevolence of non-Christian Jews whose opinion is not shared even by some of their compatriots (Ac. 23:9). Implicit in Luke's defence of Paul is the conviction that it is both natural and proper for Jewish-Christians to adhere to the law, and when it is claimed that the image of Paul the antinomian derives from the slanders of non-Christian Jews this might have received a sympathetic hearing among Jewish-Christians if they had been harassed in similar fashion too. Of course, we cannot know whether Luke intended his work to be read by his opponents or to affect his readers' attitude towards them — and it perhaps makes most sense as an attempt to set the record straight for Gentile Christian readers — but it is at least worth noting that the effect of his narrative is somewhat different if those defaming Paul are Christian rather than non-Christian Jews.

Jewish or Jewish-Christian attacks on Paul thus provide the best explanation for Luke's account of Paul and the law. It was for him a pressing and urgent issue and roughly the final third of Acts is taken up with his reply. It was one, though not necessarily the only, contemporary issue that affected his composition of Acts.

(4) We have already noted in passing that there are certain discrepancies between the Gospel and Acts on the question of the law. Perhaps the most curious is the implicit claim in Ac. 6 that Jesus spoke against neither the Temple nor the law — a claim which is difficult to maintain in the light of the sabbath disputes and the divorce saying in the Gospel. In addition, we have noted a greater degree of consistency in Acts than in the Gospel (Peter's vision is the awkward exception). It is not unnatural to conclude from this that when Luke wrote the Gospel Jesus' view of the law was not a live issue, whereas when he wrote Acts the problem of Paul and the law was. If the focus of attention when Acts was written was neither Jesus nor Peter but Paul and, to a lesser extent, the radical hellenist Stephen, this would explain why the question of 'Jesus and the law' is raised in Acts rather than in the Gospel, during the trial of Stephen rather than the trial of Jesus, and in a manner inconsistent with some of the Gospel evidence. That is, the real issue in Ac. 6 is not Jesus and the law but Stephen and the law, because Stephen, like Paul, was a radical Jewish-Christian with a reputation not dissimilar to that of Paul for attacking the law and the Temple. It is perhaps no coincidence that it is the trial of Stephen and the trial of Paul that Luke records (and not, for example the trial of Peter, presumably equally well known and probably occurring at about the same time as Paul's) and in remarkably similar fashion. Indeed it may well be that the accusations against Paul and Luke's rebuttal of them have coloured his perception of the trial of Stephen and, to a lesser extent, the trial of Jesus too.[15]

There is a further interesting shift between the Gospel and Acts in the portrayal of the Pharisees. By and large, in Acts the Pharisees are shown to be friends, or at least not the active enemies, of the Church (Ac. 5:33f; 23:1−10 cf. 26:4−6), while in the Gospel they have a more ambivalent role − sometimes the hosts (Lk. 7:36f; 11:37f; 14:2f) and allies (Lk. 13:31) of Jesus, at other times his opponents (Lk. 7:29f; 11:53f).[16] This inconsistency is the more curious because some of the anti-Pharisaic material in the Gospel seems to result from Lucan redaction. There may, however, be a simple explanation consistent with the observations made above. The surprising appearance of the Pharisees as the allies of the apostles and, more especially, of Paul, is one of the ways in which Luke defends Paul's reputation. It is surely no accident that the Pharisees were an important, if not dominant, component of the rabbinic Judaism which gradually asserted its control from Jamnia, nor that the grandson of the Gamaliel of Ac. 5 was Nasi at Jamnia during the period to which most would assign the writing of Acts.[17] When he wrote the Gospel Luke felt no need for Jesus to have the Pharisees as his allies, since his attitude towards the law was not a matter of dispute, but when he wrote Acts he needed as many supporters for Paul as he could muster. Since Paul was a Pharisee, and it was known among the Jews that he lived 'according to the strictest party' of their religion, what better witnesses of his innocence could there be than the predecessors of the leading Jews of Luke's day?

A possible, though not inevitable, conclusion to be drawn from this kind of explanation of the disparities between the Gospel and Acts is that there was a significant interval between their composition, so that similar themes could be treated somewhat differently according to the changed circumstances of Luke or his readers. There is some evidence for this in the changing view of eschatology between the Gospel and Acts,[18] the different versions of the Ascension (Lk. 24; Ac. 1) and the points of contact between Acts and the Johannine tradition,[19] and it is important at least to recognize the possibility that this was so since it can have a bearing on how we respond to the evidence of Luke's two volumes on any particular issue. Thus, for example, with regard to the question at hand, some of Jervell's arguments rest in part on the assumption that Luke's view of the law must be consistent throughout his two volumes − though they rest on his conception of Luke's overall theological scheme as well.

(5) We have noted briefly how the prophetic function of the law as scripture, which is so important to Luke's scheme of things, is developed in isolation from his assessment of the prescriptive function of the law. This creates much the same tension as in Luke's apparent assumption that Gentiles were free from the law while at the same time committed to certain fundamental beliefs and practices recommended in it. In neither

case does Luke show any awareness of the problem, so naturally he offers no solution. It is perhaps worth noting that with regard to the prophetic function of the law Luke has no qualms about recording a sharp conflict between Christians and Jews. The conflict was not over matters of practice, about which Jews and Jewish-Christians could agree, but over matters of belief. If it is true that first-century Judaism was more concerned with orthopraxy than with orthodoxy (though this may have been less true in Luke's day), Luke may deliberately be shifting the terms of the Jewish–Christian debate to the less controversial of these. To claim that Jesus was the Messiah and to attempt to prove this from scripture may not have been popular or effective among Jews but, as Akiba's assessment of Bar Cochba shows, such claims remained within the bounds of Judaism, whereas any radical departure from doing the law would have been viewed with great alarm. Yet to suppose that this was an intentional move on Luke's part, rather than simply the consequence of the expression of his Christian convictions, would involve supposing that he was interested in establishing some *rapport* with the Jews or instructing his readers how to do so. In view of his hostile depiction of the 'Jews' as the enemies of the Church and the near certainty that he wrote at a time when Church and synagogue were separate entities and relations between them strained, this seems most unlikely.

(6) Luke's view of the status of the law must also be assessed in the light of his view of the Jews and Judaism as a whole. We have noted that insofar as he has an affinity with Jewish views of the law it is with those found among hellenistic or diaspora Jews rather than those developed by the Jamnian sages after 70 C.E. This, of course, is what we would expect from an early Christian writer unless he was located in Palestine, Galilee or their immediate environs. On the one hand, the Jamnian sages, however important they are in retrospect, were at the end of the first century still in the early stages of establishing their view as *the* view of Judaism; and on the other hand, most important early Christian centres, especially after 70 C.E., were in towns where there were well-established diaspora Jewish communities. It is likely, therefore, that the types of Judaism which a Christian writer would know at first-hand were those found typically in the diaspora. Of course, we cannot draw too sharp a distinction between Jamnian and diaspora Judaism, since there is a frustrating shortage of information about the diaspora, since contacts between Jamnia and the diaspora communities were common enough, and since there were at any rate some developments after 70 C.E. which affected all forms of Judaism. There are indeed features of Luke's writings which, intentionally or not, reflect some of these changes. The picture of the Pharisees as the allies of

Paul and the other Christian leaders over against the Sadducees doubtless reflects the fate of these two groups as a result of the Jewish War. The demise of the Sadducees after 70 C.E. in conjunction with the destruction of the Temple, probably also explains why the opponents of the Church in Ac. 1—5 and 22—8 are almost always the Temple authorities and their allies. Similarly, in the speech of Stephen, insofar as either of the accusations against him is addressed, the issue of the law is dealt with positively (though the Jews are accused of failing to keep it) while the Temple is considered at greater length and in a way which may well reflect the knowledge that it had been destroyed. Further, when in the Gospel Luke shows no interest in stories which distinguish between law and tradition, a tendency confirmed by his use of ἔθος and νόμος, this may reflect the increasing dominance in Judaism of the view that placed written and unwritten Torah on a par — though it may also indicate no more than Gentile Christian indifference to a distinction which held no interest for them. Again, it may be because of the increasing dominance of Jamnian views that Luke presents Peter's vision in Ac. 10 as a challenge to Jewish law when it is, in fact, a challenge to Jewish practice based on tradition.

We might thus suppose that Luke reflects, in a variety of ways, some of the changes which took place in Judaism after the Jewish War. Of course, it would not have required an intimate knowledge of Judaism to know about the destruction of the Temple (important for Christians too) or the ascendancy of the successors of the Pharisees, so that we need not assume that Luke had particularly close contacts with Judaism. Indeed there are aspects of Judaism which he understands vaguely or not at all. The indiscriminate use of references to the 'priests', 'scribes' and 'Temple authorities' in the trial of Jesus and in Ac. 1—5; 22—8 betrays an ignorance of their precise functions and the distinctions between them, and the story in Ac. 23 shows only a vague knowledge of the conditions of a Nazirite vow or the ritual to regain levitical purity. It is worth noting, too, that later in the same chapter Luke explains the differences between Pharisees and Sadducees to his readers — which indicates that they had even less knowledge of Judaism than he had. We can conclude, therefore, that Luke seems to stand closer to hellenistic Judaism in his understanding of the law, that he reflects some of the major changes which took place in Judaism after 70 C.E. but on detailed matters sometimes goes astray. In addition to his knowledge of Judaism, however, we must now consider what his attitude towards it was.

If we concentrate on the question of law we would have to suppose that Luke was favourably disposed towards the Jews and their way of life. Since he viewed living according to the law as a natural and appropriate way of life for Jews and Jewish-Christians, and since in the Judaism of Luke's day commitment to the law had become increasingly significant, this must be considered an important and central aspect of his view of Judaism. The importance of the Jewish mission, designated by Jesus as the first responsibility of the Church and described extensively in Acts, the repeated references to large numbers of Jewish converts, and Luke's conception of the Church as the inheritor of the promises to Israel also convey a positive view of Judaism and the Jews — although in this case they are viewed as a component of the Christian movement and not as a religious entity in their own right. The same might be said of Luke's view of Jewish complicity in the death of Jesus, since although he exaggerates Jewish responsibility in the Passion narrative and in the speeches of Acts at the same time he alone among New Testament writers seems anxious to explain, if not excuse, their behaviour on the grounds of ignorance (Ac. 3:17; 13:27), and to hold out to them the offer of repentance and belief in the Gospel.[20] The assumption that the Pharisees could be favourably disposed towards Christians and find more in common with them than with the Sadducees, while it has obvious apologetic motivations, implies a positive view of one group within Judaism — a group whose views had become particularly influential in Luke's day. There is much, therefore, in Luke—Acts in addition to the material on the law which might be used to show that Luke took a positive view of Judaism, even though predictably he views it in the light of his Christian convictions.

There is, however, another and darker side to Luke's picture of the Jews. Two things in particular need to be noted. First, it is by far the majority, and probably correct, view that the stories of Jewish rejection of the gospel which leads to preaching to the Gentiles, the location of schematic statements to this effect in the three main theatres of the Pauline mission (Ac. 13:46f; 18:6; 28:28f), and the emphatic location of the last of these at the conclusion of Acts, are all indications that when Luke wrote Church and synagogue were separate entities and the Jewish mission was at an end.[21] Thus the positive side to Luke's view of Judaism, including his view of the law, and his recognition of the significance of the Jewish component in the makeup of the early Church are, from the perspective of the time of writing, largely related to the past. On the other hand, secondly, what seems to reflect Luke's present experience of Judaism are the insistent, repeated references to 'the Jews' as the enemies of the Church. The Romans oppose neither Jesus nor the apostles except under pressure from 'the Jews', and while some Jewish-Christians are alarmed at what they hear of Paul's activities, their views are either rejected or shown to be based on a misunderstanding. Paul's real opponents are always 'the Jews' and by this designation Luke seems to refer to all Jews without discrimination. Only one other document among early Christian writings, namely the Fourth Gospel, uses the label 'the Jews' in the same way to describe the enemies of the Church. It is commonly thought that one explanation for the antipathy between Christians and 'Jews' in the Fourth Gospel is the intense bitterness caused by the split between the Church and synagogue when, with the introduction of the *Birkath ha-minim* into the synagogue liturgy, Jewish-Christians were *de facto* excluded from the synagogue. In Acts there are no specific references to being 'cast out of the synagogue' as in Jn 9:22; 16:2, although the stories in Ac. 18:7 and 19:9 are of some interest in this regard;[22] but Luke may reflect a situation similar to that which apparently lies behind the Fourth Gospel, and this may explain in part the repetitive and indiscriminate use of the phrase 'the Jews' in Acts and the view of Judaism it implies.

There is thus some tension in the way Luke presents Judaism and the Jews in his narratives. We might resolve it in part by distinguishing between his view of Judaism and his view of 'the Jews'. Towards the former, as a form of religion, he remains favourably disposed — and this includes the manner in which Jewish piety is expressed through the law; whereas towards 'the Jews' who represent that religion he remains hostile. Yet this alone is an inadequate explanation and we must at least add to it a distinction between the time about which and the time at which Luke wrote. The positive aspects of Judaism and its crucial contribution to Christianity are, from Luke's point of view, largely a thing of the past. Not everything can be viewed in this way, since we must assume that Luke's positive view of Jewish legal piety, for example, extends to the time of writing. Yet the present reality for Luke and his readers was that the Jews belonged to a separate and hostile entity, the synagogue. The time for preaching to the Jews and for their acceptance of this message had passed and the Church was composed mainly of Gentiles who were active only in a Gentile mission. To this we might add, with regard to the specific question of law, that even Luke's positive account of it in Acts is designed less to propagate or legitimize legal piety as such and more to defend the beleaguered reputation of Paul.

(7) It has recently been argued that Luke's community contained a large and influential group of Jewish-Christians, separate from the synagogue but still in contact with it, for whom the problem of the Church's relation to Israel, the role of the Gentiles, and especially the reputation of Paul continued to be problematic in the face of attacks by non-Christian Jews. Only in a Jewish-Christian context, Jervell argues, can we understand the obsession of Luke with the Jewishness, including the nomism, of

Paul.[23] Jervell's assumptions about the circumstances at the time of writing appear to be correct in all but one crucial respect, namely in the identification of Luke's readers, or those among them concerned about the reputation of Paul, as Jewish-Christians. Our assessment of Luke's view of the law and Judaism has led to a reaffirmation of the common view that his readers were largely, if not exclusively, Gentiles. All the problems which Jervell attributes to the Lucan communities – the Church and Israel, Gentiles and Jews, Paul and the law – could have been as pressing for Pauline Gentile Christians as for Jewish-Christians, and much of the material which might seem to be upholding Jewish practices is, as it were, a by-product of the more central defence of Paul. Indeed, there is not even any need to assume, as O'Neill does,[24] that Luke's communities contained a Jewish-Christian minority, much the same as described in Justin's *Dialogue* 47, who had worked out a compromise with the Gentile Christian majority whereby they retained their right to live according to the Jewish law in exchange for their recognition that Gentile Christians should be free from most of it – a compromise which is both recognized and authorized by the narrative of Acts. We cannot of course be certain, but there is no pressing evidence which demands that we assume a significant Jewish-Christian component (majority or minority) in the Lucan communities, and there is much that speaks against it.

The communities for whom Luke wrote, it would appear, were mainly Gentile, experienced non-Christian Judaism as a hostile force, and may have known of Jewish-Christian anti-Paulinism as well. This broad profile fits almost any of the main areas where Christian communities had become established by the end of the first century and provides us with nothing very substantial with which to choose between Rome, Asia Minor and Antioch – the three main options for the place of composition of Acts. And even if we could be more confident on this score, it is doubtful that we know enough about any of these areas that would help us to describe the situation of Luke more precisely.

NOTES

1 Legal terminology in Luke–Acts

1 H. Kleinknecht and W. Gutbrod, art. νόμος, *TDNT*, vol. IV, pp. 1022–91. For Luke see J. Jervell, *Luke and the People of God* (Minneapolis, 1972), pp. 136–7.

2 H. Conzelmann, *The Theology of Saint Luke* (London, 1961), pp. 57–9, discusses the connection between the Transfiguration and the Passion.

3 E.E. Ellis, *St. Luke* (London, 1966), p. 143; A.R.C. Leaney, *The Gospel According to St. Luke* (London, 1958), p. 168.

4 For contrasting assessments of possible christological allusions see Conzelmann, *Luke*, p. 166 n. 2 and R.C. Zehnle, *Peter's Pentecost Discourse* (New York, 1971), pp. 76f.

5 Jervell, *Luke*, p. 137.

6 W. Meeks, *The Prophet-King. Moses in Johannine Christology* (Leiden, 1967), pp. 113–30, 132–3.

7 W.D. Davies, *The Setting of the Sermon on the Mount* (Cambridge, 1964), pp. 184f.

8 H. Conzelmann, *Die Apostelgeschichte* (Tübingen, 1963), p. 48; E. Haenchen, *The Acts of the Apostles* (Oxford, 1971), p. 283.

9 SB, vol. III, pp. 554f.

10 E. Richard, *Acts 6:1–8:4. The Author's Method of Composition* (Missoula, 1978), p. 291, prefers the general sense 'ancestral custom', as against 'torah legislation', in Ac. 15:1; 21:21, but recognizes the latter sense in Ac. 6:14. H. Preisker, *TDNT*, vol. II, pp. 372–3 thinks ἔθος refers to the cultic laws of Moses. L. Goppelt, *Christentum und Judentum im ersten und zweiten Jahrhundert* (Gütersloh, 1954), pp. 231–3, suggests that Luke distinguishes between the law in general (νόμος) and its ceremonial aspects in particular (ἔθος) and thereby tries to show the Church what parts of the law are still applicable to their moral behaviour. As we have seen, however, Luke's usage suggests that for him the terms were synonymous.

11 Z.W. Falk, *Introduction to Jewish Law of the Second Commonwealth* (Leiden, 1972), pp. 15f; Peter Richardson, ' "I say, not the Lord": Personal Opinion, Apostolic Authority and the Development of Early Christian Halakah', *Tyndale Bulletin* 31 (1980), 65–86, here 74–9.

12 Falk, *Law*, p. 15.

13 Falk, *Law*, p. 15.
14 W. Gutbrod, art. νόμος, *TDNT*, vol. IV, pp. 1050–1.
15 J.N. Sevenster, *The Roots of Pagan Anti-Semitism in the Ancient World* (Leiden, 1975), especially pp. 89–144. For the relevant texts see especially the collection by M. Stern, *Greek and Latin Authors on Jews and Judaism*, vols. I and II (Jerusalem, 1976, 1980).
16 See also G. Delling, 'Josephus und die heidnischen Religionen', *Klio* 43–4 (1965), 263–9.
17 Jervell, *Luke*, p. 137.

2 Law in Luke's Gospel

1 R. Banks, *Jesus and the Law in the Synoptic Tradition* (Cambridge, 1975), pp. 215–16, lists the options.
2 H. Hübner, *Das Gesetz in der synoptischen Tradition* (Witten, 1973), pp. 16–19.
3 J.M. Creed, *The Gospel according to St. Luke* (London, 1942), p. 151; W. Grundmann, *Das Evangelium nach Lukas* (Berlin, 1966), p. 222; R. Bultmann, *The History of the Synoptic Tradition* (Oxford, 1968), pp. 22–3, 51.
4 K.H. Rengstorf, *Das Evangelium nach Lukas* (Göttingen, 1966), p. 138; Ellis, *Luke*, p. 158.
5 Banks, *Law*, p. 165; E. Haenchen, *Der Weg Jesu* (Berlin, 1966), pp. 413–14; T. Schramm, *Der Markus-Stoff bei Lukas* (Cambridge, 1971), pp. 47f.
6 B.S. Easton, *The Gospel According to St. Luke* (Edinburgh, 1926), p. 169.
7 Easton, *Luke*, p. 169; Haenchen, *Weg*, p. 414.
8 Banks, *Law*, p. 166.
9 J. Fichtner, art. πλησίον, *TDNT*, vol. VI, pp. 311f; SB, vol. I, pp. 357f.
10 Cf. Rengstorf, *Lukas*, pp. 138–9.
11 K. Berger, *Die Gesetzauslegung Jesu* (Neukirchen-Vluyn, 1972), pp. 233–9. On the historical problem of the love commands see his lengthy discussion on pp. 56–257.
12 G. Sellin, 'Lukas als Gleichniserzähler: Die Erzählung vom barmherzigen Samariter (Lk. 10:25–37)', *ZNW* 66 (1975), 19–60.
13 Sellin, 'Lukas', p. 23 n. 117.
14 Sellin, 'Lukas', pp. 42–3.
15 Easton, *Luke*, p. 255.
16 Berger, *Gesetzauslegung*, p. 50.
17 Berger, *ibid.*
18 J. Schniewind, *Das Evangelium nach Matthäus* (Göttingen, 1950), p. 238.
19 Easton, *Luke*, p. 189.
20 Banks, *Law*, p. 179.
21 Omitted by D and Marcion. Several MSS read χρηστός in place of χρηστότερος.

22 H. Schürmann, *Das Lukasevangelium* (Freiburg, 1969), part I, pp. 298f.

23 Grundmann, *Lukas*, pp. 133–4.

24 H.J. Kraus, 'Freude an Gottes Gesetz', *Ev. Th.* 11 (1950–1), 337–51; A. Plummer, *The Gospel According to St. Luke* (Edinburgh, 1910), p. 9.

25 Grundmann, *Lukas*, p. 67 for details.

26 Easton, *Luke*, p. 26, follows D, but is virtually alone in this. See Creed, *Luke*, p. 39; Schürmann, *Lukasevangelium*, pp. 121–2.

27 SB, vol. II, pp. 144–7.

28 See the survey in Schürmann, *Lukasevangelium*, pp. 144f.

29 P.S. Minear, 'Luke's Use of the Birth Stories', *SLA*, pp. 111f; H.H. Oliver, 'The Lukan Birth Stories and the Purpose of Luke–Acts', *NTS* 10 (1963–4), 202f.

30 Plummer, *Luke*, p. 118; B.H. Branscomb, *Jesus and the Law of Moses* (New York, 1930), p. 127.

31 Banks, *Law*, pp. 91–2; Ellis, *Luke*, p. 96.

32 See Banks, *Law*, p. 103 and literature cited; H. Strathmann, art. μαρτύριον, *TDNT*, vol. IV, pp. 502–3.

33 Plummer, *Luke*, p. 150.

34 Schürmann, *Lukasevangelium*, p. 277.

35 *Contra* Plummer, *Luke*, p. 312; Creed, *Luke*, p. 167.

36 E.g. Ellis, *Luke*, pp. 170–2.

37 S.G. Wilson, *The Gentiles and the Gentile Mission in Luke–Acts* (Cambridge, 1973), pp. 66, 243f.

38 W. Wagner, 'In Welcher Sinne hat Jesus das Prädikat ἀγαθός von sich abgewiesen?', *ZNW* 8 (1907), 143–61; Berger, *Gesetzauslegung*, pp. 398–401.

39 See the discussion by Berger, *Gesetzauslegung*, pp. 362–95. He refers to 1QS 8:2; Sib. Or. 3:324–47; Jub. 7:20; 36:3f; Test. Iss. 7:3–6; Test. Ben. 4; Tob. 4:5–19; Matt. 25:35–9; 42–5; Arist. *Apol.* XIV.2–3. The same approach is found throughout Philo *Virt.* 51f and Jos. *Ant.* IV.180f. Typical is the concern for the obligations of rulers or other individuals towards strangers or the disadvantaged (widows, poor, oppressed, etc.). These summaries are frequently bracketed by an initial reference to doing righteousness (or not doing unrighteousness) and a concluding comment on relations with God and are thus linked to the similar phenomenon discussed below in ch. 3 n. 22. The evidence comes from Palestinian and diaspora Judaism but, Berger argues, in the latter they tend to serve as a substitute for, or summary of, the whole law.

40 E.g. Berger, *Gesetzauslegung*, pp. 396f.

41 Berger, *ibid.*, pp. 429f.

42 Berger, *ibid.*, pp. 433f, comes close to this without connecting it with Lk. 10.

43 Conzelmann, *Luke*, p. 23, cf. pp. 160, 185.

44 Grundmann, *Lukas*, p. 135; Leaney, *Luke*, p. 130.

45 Plummer, *Luke*, p. 166. See the recent discussion by G.W.

Buchanan and C. Wolfe, 'The "Second-First Sabbath" (Lk. 6:1)', *JBL* 97 (1978), 259–62; and I.H. Marshall, *The Gospel of Luke* (Exeter, 1978), p. 230.

46 Hübner, *Gesetz*, pp. 117–19.
47 SB, vol. I, pp. 618f.
48 D. Daube, 'Responsibilities of Master and Disciples in the Gospels', *NTS* 19 (1972), 1f.
49 SB, vol. I, pp. 618f.
50 SB, vol. I, pp. 623f; II, pp. 533f.
51 *Contra* Easton, *Luke*, p. 74.
52 Cf. Leaney, *Luke*, p. 131; Rengstorf, *Lukas*, p. 81.
53 D. Daube, *The New Testament and Rabbinic Judaism* (London, 1956), p. 68.
54 *Contra* Branscomb, *Law*, p. 146; Ellis, *Luke*, p. 109.
55 Banks, *Law*, pp. 121–2; Schürmann, *Lukasevangelium*, pp. 303–5.
56 Hübner, *Gesetz*, pp. 119f; Haenchen, *Weg*, pp. 120–2; E. Lohse, art. σάββατον, *TDNT*, vol. VII, p. 23.
57 Banks, *Law*, pp. 116–17.
58 Banks, *Law*, p. 122 and notes.
59 Haenchen, *Weg*, p. 121.
60 Schürmann, *Lukasevangelium*, p. 304.
61 Banks, *Law*, p. 120; Schürmann, *Lukasevangelium*, pp. 304–5.
62 Cf. W. Käser, 'Exegetische Erwägungen zur Seligpreisung des Sabbatarbeiters Lk. 6:5 D', *ZNW* 65 (1968), 414–30.
63 Banks, *Law*, p. 121; Grundmann, *Lukas*, pp. 135–6; J. Schmid, *Das Evangelium nach Lukas* (Regensburg, 1960), p. 127.
64 SB, vol. I, pp. 623–9; I. Abrahams, *Studies in Pharisaism and the Gospels* (Cambridge, 1917), vol. I, pp. 129–35.
65 Banks, *Law*, p. 125.
66 Perhaps 'son', as in some MSS, since it is the *lectio difficilior* and may be the result of mistranslation of an Aramaic original – see M. Black, *An Aramaic Approach to the Gospel and Acts* (Oxford, 1967), pp. 168f.
67 SB, vol. I, pp. 629–30.
68 SB, vol. I, pp. 629f; II, pp. 199f.
69 Banks, *Law*, pp. 129–30.
70 E. Lohse, art. σάββατον, *TDNT*, vol. VII, pp. 1–10. The best account is R. Goldenberg, 'The Jewish Sabbath in the Roman World up to the time of Constantine the Great', *ANRW*, II.19.1, pp. 414–47.
71 Lohse, art. σάββατον, pp. 29–34; Goldenberg, 'Sabbath', pp. 442f.
72 Banks, *Law*, pp. 130–1.
73 *Contra* Ellis, *Luke*, p. 186.
74 This may not, of course, be an accurate record of how Jesus engaged in debate with his contemporaries, though in either case the suggestion of Neusner, that R. Eliezer's reform of the sabbath law after 70 C.E. is equivalent to the programme implied in Lk.

6:5 pars., seems strained. For the Gospel writers, at least, Jesus' claim is more radical and has more extensive ramifications than anything attributed to Eliezer. See J. Neusner, 'The Formation of Rabbinic Judaism: Javneh (Jamnia) from AD 70–100', *ANRW*, II.19.2, pp. 3–42, here p. 33. Further discussion of Jesus' view of the sabbath can be found in S. Westerholm, *Jesus and Scribal Authority* (Lund, 1978), pp. 92f.

75 M. Hengel, *Charisma und Nachfolge* (Berlin, 1968), pp. 3–17; Banks, *Law*, p. 97.

76 *Contra* Banks, *Law*, p. 97.

77 SB, vol. I, p. 495; Abrahams, *Studies*, vol. I, pp. 139–49; R. Bultmann, art. ἀφιέναι, *TDNT*, vol. I, pp. 509–12; C.G. Montefiore, *Rabbinic Literature and Gospel Teachings* (New York, 1970), p. 221.

78 SB, vol. I, pp. 1010f; H.W. Beyer, art. βλασφημία, *TDNT*, vol. I, pp. 621–5.

79 J. Neusner, *Rabbinic Traditions About the Pharisees before 70* (Leiden, 1971).

80 SB, vol. II, pp. 495–519; Abrahams, *Studies*, vol. I, pp. 55f; G.F. Moore, *Judaism in the First Centuries of the Christian Era* (Cambridge, 1930), vol. II, pp. 70–8, 156–61.

81 Conzelmann, *Luke*, pp. 99–101.

82 S. Schulz, 'Markus und das Alte Testament', *ZTK* 58 (1961), 184f, here 190; similarly Branscomb, *Law*, p. 135.

83 Banks, *Law*, p. 111.

84 E.g. Daube, *Judaism*, pp. 292f; E. Rodenbusch, 'Die Komposition von Lucas 16', *ZNW* 4 (1903), 241–54; Easton, *Luke*, p. 244; H. Schürmann, *Traditionsgeschichtliche Untersuchungen zu den synoptischen Evangelien* (Düsseldorf, 1968), pp. 127f.

85 See W.G. Kümmel, *Promise and Fulfilment* (London, 1957), pp. 121f and literature cited there.

86 Berger, *Gesetzauslegung*, pp. 209–26; similarly Conzelmann, *Luke*, pp. 158–61, 185 n. 4.

87 Wilson, *Gentiles*, pp. 78–9.

88 Banks, *Law*, p. 213; Hübner, *Gesetz*, pp. 15f; H.T. Wrege, *Die Überlieferungsgeschichte der Bergpredigt* (Tübingen, 1968), pp. 38f.

89 Plummer, *Luke*, pp. 388–9.

90 H.A.W. Meyer, *A Critical and Exegetical Commentary on the New Testament* (Edinburgh, 1885), p. 231; for a summary of other views see Banks, *Law*, p. 214 n. 2.

91 Wrege, *Bergpredigt*, pp. 39–40; Hübner, *Gesetz*, pp. 17f.

92 Banks, *Law*, pp. 215f.

93 See for example G. Delling, 'Das Logion Mk. 10:11 (und seine Abwandlung) im N.T.', *NT* 1 (1956), 263–74; H. Greeven, 'Ehe nach dem N.T.', *NTS* 15 (1968–9), 365–88; and the long discussions in Hübner, *Gesetz*, pp. 42f; Berger, *Gesetzauslegung*, pp. 508f; and Westerholm, *Scribal*, pp. 114f.

94 See J.A. Fitzmyer, 'The Matthean Divorce Texts and some new

Palestinian Evidence', *Theol. Stud.* 37 (1976), 197–226; J.R. Mueller, 'The Temple Scroll and the Gospel Divorce Texts', *Rev. Qum.* 10 (1980), 247–56.

95 Conzelmann, *Luke*, pp. 23, 158f, 185, quotation p. 161.
96 Berger, *Gesetzauslegung*, pp. 222–6.
97 Daube, *Judaism*, pp. 292f; Leaney, *Luke*, p. 224.
98 J.D.M. Derrett, *Law in the New Testament* (London, 1970), pp. 82–5.
99 Schürmann, *Untersuchungen*, pp. 126–36.
100 Hübner, *Gesetz*, pp. 22f.
101 Banks, *Law*, pp. 214f.
102 Similarly Marshall, *Luke*, pp. 630–2; G. Schneider, *Das Evangelium nach Lukas* (Gütersloh, 1977), pp. 336–9. Banks discusses Lk. 16:18 separately from verses 16–17.
103 Cf. Grundmann, *Lukas*, p. 324, who assumes a similar understanding among Luke's readers.
104 B.H. Streeter, *The Four Gospels* (London, 1924), pp. 176f.
105 Conzelmann, *Luke*, pp. 52–5; V. Taylor, *Behind the Third Gospel* (London, 1926), p. 91.
106 Schürmann, *Untersuchungen*, pp. 272–89; *idem. Lukasevangelium*, pp. 525f.
107 Hübner, *Gesetz*, pp. 184f.
108 Conzelmann, *Luke*, pp. 23, 158–61, 185 n. 4.
109 Hübner, *Gesetz*, pp. 207–11.
110 Jervell, *Luke*, pp. 138f, quotation p. 141.
111 Banks, *Law*, pp. 172, 246–8.
112 On hellenistic Jewish assessments of the law see Berger, *Gesetzauslegung*, pp. 38–55.

3 The law in Acts

1 E.g. Lake and Cadbury, *BC*, vol. IV, p. 157.
2 Haenchen, *Acts*, p. 446, n. 3; Conzelmann, *Apostelgeschichte*, pp. 77, 83.
3 J.L. Nolland, 'A Fresh Look at Acts 15:10', *NTS* 27 (1980), 105.
4 Conzelmann, *Apostelgeschichte*, p. 83. The observation goes back to F. Overbeck in his revision of W.M.L. de Wette's *Kurze Erklärung der Apostelgeschichte* (Leipzig, 1870), p. 226.
5 Jervell, *Luke*, p. 144. On p. 141 he claims that 'Luke has the most conservative outlook within the New Testament.'
6 P. Vielhauer, 'On the "Paulinism" of Acts', *SLA*, pp. 51f, here p. 44.
7 Jervell, *Luke*, pp. 138–40, exaggerates this aspect of Acts 1–8.
8 See S.G. Wilson, 'The Death of Jesus and the Jews in Acts', in *Early Christian Anti-Judaism*, vol. I, ed. G.P. Richardson, D. Granskou (forthcoming).
9 Jervell, *Luke*, pp. 138–40.
10 SB, vol. IV/1, pp. 378f, 383; vol. II, pp. 376f.
11 E.g. Haenchen, *Acts*, pp. 478–82. Conzelmann, *Apostelgeschichte*, p. 89.

12 Haenchen, *Acts*, p. 481, quoting Overbeck, *Kurze*, p. 250.
13 V. Stolle, *Die Zeuge als Angeklagter* (Stuttgart, 1973), pp. 76–8.
14 Haenchen, *Acts*, pp. 611–14; followed by I.H. Marshall, *Acts* (Leicester, 1980), p. 345 n. 1.
15 Haenchen, *Acts*, p. 639.
16 It should be noted that many dispute Josephus' statement.
17 The shift from 'common' (κοινός) food to 'common' people is found in IV Macc. 7:6. Cf. W. Paschen, *Rein und Unrein* (Munich, 1970), pp. 166–8.
18 Sevenster, *Anti-Semitism*, pp. 89f.
19 G. Alon, *Jews and Judaism in the Classical World* (Jerusalem, 1977), pp. 146–89 argues that they were. For a different assessment see S. Zeitlin, 'Proselytes and Proselytism during the Second Commonwealth and the early Tannaitic Period', in *Studies in the Early History of Judaism* (New York, 1974), vol. II, pp. 407–17. The problem with the argument in both cases is that the bulk of the evidence is rabbinic and difficult to date.
20 A point made by Alon, *ibid.*, pp. 157, 189 and SB, vol. IV, p. 353. It should be noted that many of the examples quoted above, especially with regard to food, are associated with periods when Judaism was under unusual stress (such as the Maccabean rebellion) and may not reflect normal, everyday practice.
21 A point made by F. Siegert, 'Gottesfürchtige und Sympathisenten', *JSJ* 4 (1973), 109–64, here 131–2.
22 Berger, *Gesetzauslegung*, pp. 141f, 362f. See also N.J. McEleney, 'Conversion, Circumcision and the Law', *NTS* 20 (1973–4), 319–40, here 323f; R.A. Horsley, 'Gnosis in Corinth', *NTS* 27 (1980), 32–51, here 41f. Apart from the example quoted, summaries of the law, especially in twofold form, are common in Philo (*Abr.* 208; *Vit. Mos.* II.163; *Virt.* 54, 95; *Q.E.* II.2; *Dec.* 110–11), and typically in terms of εὐσέβεια and φιλανθρωπία. Josephus does the same, though he normally uses εὐσέβεια and δικαιοσύνη (*Ant.* I.2; X.50; XII.284; XV.374f; *Ap.* II.291). Summarizing the law is not entirely unknown in rabbinic literature (see, for example, Hillel's dicta) but it is not typical. It is most common in hellenistic Judaism, where it often has an apologetic motivation: to make the law intelligible to non-Jews by reducing it to its basic principles (Philo *Spec. Leg.* II.62–3) or to show that Jews were not ἀθέους καὶ μισανθρώπους (Jos. *Ap.* II.148). See above ch. 2 n. 39.
23 A Harnack, *The Acts of the Apostles* (London, 1939), p. 255 n. 3, formulates this tension clearly.
24 H. Diehl, 'Das sogenannte Aposteldekret. Ein Beitrag zum Kritik von A. Harnack's "Apostelgeschichte" ', *ZNW* 10 (1909), 277–96, here 286.
25 M. Wilcox, 'The "God-Fearers" in Acts – A Reconsideration', *JSNT* 13 (1981), 102–22, has recently argued that 'godfearer' is not a technical term in Acts and that it refers to 'the pious', whether Jew or Gentile, proselyte or 'adherent'. A similar point

is made by McEleney, 'Conversion', pp. 325f. I have continued to use the term in the more traditional way but their arguments, if correct, would reinforce the general drift of my argument.

26 E.g. Haenchen, *Acts*, p. 354; Conzelmann, *Apostelgeschichte*, p. 66.
27 Haenchen, *Acts*, p. 450 n. 1.
28 On the Noachic laws see below.
29 J.C. O'Neill, *The Theology of Acts in its Historical Setting*, 2nd ed. rev. (London, 1970), p. 108.
30 O'Neill, *Acts*, pp. 106–8.
31 J. Weiss, *Earliest Christianity* (Gloucester, 1970), vol. I, p. 131.
32 A common view, perhaps most strongly stated in M. Dibelius, *Studies in the Acts of the Apostles* (London, 1956), pp. 109f.
33 A. Steinemann, *Die Apostelgeschichte* (Bern, 1934), p. 164; O'Neill, *Acts* (1st ed.), pp. 101–2.
34 So. W. Schmithals, *Paul and James* (London, 1965), pp. 97f; disputed by O'Neill, *Acts* (2nd ed.), pp. 107–8.
35 As argued by D. Catchpole, 'Paul, James and Apostolic Decree', *NTS* 23 (1976–7), 428–44.
36 See above all J.C. Hurd Jnr, *The Origin of I Corinthians* (London, 1965). Also T.W. Manson, 'The Corinthian Correspondence (1) and (2)', in *Studies in the Gospels and Epistles* (Manchester, 1962), ed. M. Black, pp. 190–224, here p. 200.
37 For a full list see W.G. Kümmel, 'Die älteste Form des Apostel-dekrets', in *Heilgeschehen und Geschichte: Gesammelte Aufsätze, 1933–64* (Marburg, 1965), pp. 278–88, here pp. 278f.
38 A.F.J. Klijn, *A Survey of the Researches into the Western Text of The Gospel and Acts: Part 2, 1949–69* (Leiden, 1969), pp. 64–5. See recently C.M. Martini, 'La Tradition textuelle des Actes des Apôtres', in *Les Actes des Apôtres: Tradition, Redaction, Théologie* (Louvain, 1979), ed. J. Kremer; and in the same volume M. Wilcox, 'Luke and the Bezan Text of Acts', pp. 447–55. Wilcox concludes that the 'Lucan' flavour of Codex Bezae means that we must take seriously all the individual readings within it.
39 See Kümmel, 'Aposteldekret', pp. 279f.
40 K. Aland, *Studien zur Überlieferung des Neuen Testaments und seines Textes* (Berlin, 1967), pp. 155–72; Haenchen, *Acts*, pp. 56f.
41 See below for detailed discussion of the terms of the decree.
42 Substantially the view of J.H. Ropes, *BC*, vol. III, pp. 265f; followed by K. Lake, *BC*, vol. V, pp. 195f. They think the original decree was threefold and cultic. The threefold form is found in Tertullian (*De Pud.* 12) but is taken in an ethical sense even though Tertullian is elsewhere aware of the prohibition against idol-food, blood, strangled things and fornication. Even if we impugn Tertullian as a witness (so Kümmel) the possibility remains that either the Lucan or the original form of the decree contained three rather than four terms.

43 See the discussion on pp. 96f below.

44 See further Harnack, *Acts*, pp. 257–8.

45 SB, vol. IV/1, pp. 353f categorizes the Jewish view of non-Jews under these three headings: they are idolators, shedders of blood and immoral. According to Conzelmann, *Apostelgeschichte*, pp. 84–5, this evidence is used by G. Strothotte to argue that the decree originally had an ethical sense (unpublished dissertation (Erlangen, 1955), entitled 'Das Apostelkonzil im Lichte der jüdischen Rechtsgeschichte').

46 E.J. Epp, *The Theological Tendency of Codex Bezae Cantabrigiensis* (Cambridge, 1966).

47 C.K. Barrett, 'Is there a theological tendency in Codex Bezae?', in *Text and Interpretation* (Cambridge, 1979), ed. E. Best and R.McL. Wilson, pp. 15–28.

48 Klijn, *Survey*, pp. 66f.

49 So Lake and Cadbury, *BC*, vol. IV, p. 177.

50 See Lake and Cadbury, *BC*, vol. IV, pp. 180–1.

51 J.H. Moulton and G. Milligan, *The Vocabulary of the Greek New Testament* (London, 1930), pp. 228–9.

52 Jervell, *Luke*, p. 144.

53 On φυλάσσειν see G. Bertram, *TDNT*, vol. IX, pp. 236f, and in relation to the law see Lk. 18:11 pars., Ac. 7:53; 21:24. The only other use of διατηρείν in the New Testament is Lk. 2:51, which has nothing to do with the law.

54 Lake and Cadbury, *BC*, vol. IV, p. 174.

55 Nolland, 'Acts 15:10', pp. 105f.

56 Lake and Cadbury, *BC*, vol. IV, pp. 177–8, following J.H. Ropes in *JBL* 15 (1896), 75–81. See also Dibelius, *Studies*, p. 98 and E. Franklin, *Christ the Lord* (London, 1975), p. 128.

57 Franklin, *Christ*, *loc. cit.*

58 So Haenchen, *Acts*, p. 450; Conzelmann, *Apostelgeschichte*, p. 85.

59 Lake and Cadbury, *BC*, vol. IV, p. 178.

60 Argued or assumed by the majority of modern commentators on Acts. See commentaries *ad loc.*

61 The conversion of King Izates again comes to mind. See further in K.G. Kuhn, art. προσήλυτος, *TDNT*, vol. VI, p. 731.

62 Haenchen, *Acts*, p. 449.

63 Haenchen, *Acts*, p. 469.

64 Kuhn, art. προσήλυτος, pp. 725–44.

65 See Sanh. 56*b* and compare the similar material in Sib. Or. 4:28f.

66 Siegert, 'Gottesfürchtige', pp. 120–1 thinks they probably were.

67 So M. Simon, 'The Apostolic Decree and its Setting in the Ancient Church', *BJRL* 52 (1969–70), 437–60, here 444f.

68 Kuhn, art. cit., p. 741; SB, vol. II, p. 722.

69 SB, vol. II, pp. 729f; Haenchen, *Acts*, p. 449; O'Neill, *Acts* (2nd ed.), pp. 106f.

70 F. Hauck and S. Schulz, art. πόρνη, *TDNT*, vol. VI, pp. 579f.

71 Haenchen, *Acts*, p. 449 n. 5.

72 The best discussion of πυκτός is by H. Bietenhard, art. πυκτός, *TDNT*, vol. VI, pp. 455–8.

73 SB, vol. II, pp. 730–4.

74 Most effectively pointed out by G. Resch, *Das Aposteldekret* (Leipzig, 1905), *TU*, NS 13.

75 Bauer, *Lexicon*, p. 686.

76 R. Herzog, 'Aus dem Asklepeion von Kos', *ARW* 10 (1907), 400–15.

77 H. Lietzmann, 'Der Sinn des Aposteldekrets und seine Text-wandlung', in *Amicitiae Corolla* (London, 1933), ed. H.G. Wood, pp. 203–11, here pp. 205–6.

78 The view of Bietenhard, art. πυκτός, p. 458, following Strothotte (above n. 45). The traditional association of the Neutral text with Alexandria and the reference in Philo *Spec. Leg.* IV.122 presumably dictate the choice of Alexandria. Neither is in fact a strong argument, but the precise location is of little significance for this point. For a similar view see Resch, *Das Aposteldekret*, pp. 153f.

79 P.W. van der Horst, *The Sentences of Pseudo-Phocylides* (Leiden, 1978), pp. 135–6, considers no. 31 to be a later, Christian addition under the influence of the decree in Acts.

80 C.K. Barrett, 'Things Sacrificed to Idols', *NTS* 11 (1964–5), 138–52, here 144–6; H. Conzelmann, *I Corinthians* (Philadelphia, 1975), pp. 176–7.

81 H. Lietzmann, *An die Korinther I und II* (Tübingen, 1949), pp. 49–52.

82 A. Ehrhardt, 'Social Problems in the Early Church: 1. The Sunday Joint of the Christian Housewife', in *The Framework of the New Testament Stories* (Manchester, 1964), pp. 276–90.

83 H. von Campenhausen, *The Formation of the Christian Bible* (Philadelphia, 1972), pp. 37f.

84 K. Lake, *BC*, vol. V, pp. 205f.

85 Kümmel, 'Aposteldekret', pp. 285–7; similarly Siegert, 'Gottes-fürchtige', p. 135.

86 See recently Horsley, 'Gnosis', pp. 41f.

87 Barrett, 'Idols', pp. 139–40; Simon, 'Decree', p. 442.

88 Kümmel, 'Aposteldekret', pp. 285–6.

89 That πορνεία may be covered by the ablution rules in the Pseudo-Clementines is argued by E. Molland, 'La Circoncision, le Baptême et l'Autorité du Décret Apostolique (Actes 15:28 seq.) dans les Milieux Judéo-Chrétiens des Pseudo-Clémentines', *Stud. Theol.* 8 (1955), 1–39. A.F.J. Klijn disputes this in 'The Pseudo-Clementines and the Apostolic Decree', *NT* 10 (1968), 305–12.

90 G. Strecker, *Das Judenchristentum in den Pseudoklementinen* (Berlin, 1958), *TU* 70, pp. 70–2.

91 So Klijn, 'Decree', pp. 310–12. He believes that the *Grundschrift* prohibited the 'tables of demons' and 'blood' and that these were later reinterpreted by, among other things, the terms of the decree.

92 Untangling sources and traditions within the Pseudo-Clementines

remains an uncertain business despite the impressive work of Strecker.

93 F. Hauck and S. Schulz, art. πόρνη, *TDNT*, vol. VI, pp. 579f, here pp. 581f (with literature). See also G.D. Fee, 'εἰδωλόθυτα Once again. I Cor. 9–10', *Biblica* 61 (1980), 172–97. Cf. Jos. *Ant.* XVIII.65–8.

94 On pagan cult practices in general see the articles in PW under *Opfer* (XVIII.1, pp. 579–627), *Trankopfer* (VI.A.2, pp. 2131f), *Immolatio* (IX.1, pp. 1112–33) and their bibliographies. The substantial works on cultic and sacrificial practices used in these articles have not been superseded.

95 This is how Resch, *Das Aposteldekret*, pp. 160f, explains the introduction of πνικτός into the decree in Alexandria *c.* 200 C.E. For other historical examples of the strangling of sacrificial animals see K. Meuli, 'Griechische Opferbräuche', in *Phyllobolia* (Basel, 1945), ed. O. Gigon, K. Meuli, W. Theiler, F. Wehrli, B. Wyss.

96 Line 30 has an interesting allusion to the statue of a youth 'strangling a goose' – but whether he represents a god and whether his action is cultic remain unclear.

97 Quoted in H.A.W. Meyer, *Critical and Exegetical Handbook to the Acts of the Apostles* (New York, 1883), p. 290 (original unavailable).

98 See further PW *Opfer* (above n. 94), pp. 613–21, *Immolatio*, pp. 1130–3; also Meuli, 'Opfergebräuche', pp. 268f with parallels.

99 SB, vol. IV, pp. 353f.

4 Law, Judaism and the Gentiles

1 O'Neill, *Acts* (2nd ed.), pp. 139f and especially Sellin, 'Lukas', pp. 52f. On Acts 7 see M. Simon, *St. Stephen and the Hellenists* (London, 1956), pp. 100f; U. Wilckens, *Die Missionsreden der Apostelgeschichte*, 3rd rev. ed. (Neukirchen-Vluyn, 1970), pp. 109–37, 193–224.

2 E.g. W. Nauck, 'Die Tradition und Komposition der Areopagrede', *ZTK* 53 (1956), 11f; H. Conzelmann, 'The Address of Paul on the Areopagus', *SLA*, pp. 225–7.

3 Wilson, *Gentiles*, pp. 217–18; *Luke and the Pastoral Epistles* (London, 1979), pp. 33–4.

4 E. Haenchen, 'Judentum und Christentum in der Apostel- geschichte', *ZNW* 54 (1963), 155f.

5 Jervell, *Luke*, p. 143.

6 The key essay is 'The Divided People of God', *Luke*, pp. 41–74. For a critique see Wilson, *Gentiles*, pp. 219f.

7 Jervell recognizes this too (*Luke*, p. 68), despite his emphasis on the Jewishness of Luke's Church. See recently H.J. Hauser, *Strukturen der Abschlusserzählung der Apostelgeschichte (Apg. 28:16–31)* (Rome, 1979), pp. 81f, 240–1.

8 *Contra* Jervell, *Luke*, pp. 146–7, 176–7; O'Neill, *Acts* (2nd ed.), pp. 113f.

9 Jervell, *Luke*, p. 146: 'Paul is Luke's real problem.'

10 See L. Gaston, 'Anti-Judaism and the Passion Narrative in Luke–Acts', in *Anti-Judaism in Early Christianity*, ed. G.P. Richardson and D. Granskou (forthcoming).

11 Jervell, *Luke*, pp. 185f.

12 E.g. E. Trocmé, *Le 'Livre des Actes' et l'Histoire* (Paris, 1957), pp. 53f.

13 Notably Jervell, *Luke*, pp. 146–7, 176–7.

14 Fragment of Stephanus Gobarus, acc. to Photius, *Library*, codex 232. Quoted in W. Bauer, *Orthodoxy and Heresy in Earliest Christianity* (Philadelphia, 1971), p. 214 n. 33. But see the comments of C.K. Barrett in 'Pauline Controversies in the Post-Pauline Period', *NTS* 20 (1973–4), 229–45, here 236. This article and A. Lindemann, *Paulus im ältesten Christentum* (Tübingen, 1979), contain further information on the reaction to Paul.

15 S.G. Wilson, 'The Death of Jesus and the Jews in Acts', in forthcoming volume listed above (n. 10).

16 J.A. Ziesler, 'Luke and the Pharisees', *NTS* 25 (1979), 146–57.

17 Gaston, *art. cit.* (n. 10).

18 Wilson, *Gentiles*, pp. 81f.

19 F.L. Cribbs, 'Agreements between John and Acts', in *Perspectives on Luke–Acts* (Danville, 1978), ed. C.H. Talbert, pp. 40–61, here p. 61.

20 E.g. Ac. 2:38; 3:19f; 10:43; 13:38.

21 Above n. 7. This view is widely held despite differing assessments of the number and significance of Jewish and Gentile Christians in Luke's communities.

22 O'Neill, *Acts* (2nd ed.), pp. 133f, argues, for somewhat different reasons, for a similar setting, i.e. after the introduction of the *Birkath ha-minim*.

23 Jervell, *Luke*, pp. 146–7, 176–7, contrasting Luke's situation where Jewish-Christians are a sizeable group, if not a majority, with that of Justin *Dial.* 47 where Jewish-Christians are clearly a minority.

24 O'Neill, *Acts* (2nd ed.), pp. 113f, arguing that the situation is identical to that of Justin *Dial.* 47, where Jewish-Christians are a minority, and that the only difference is that Justin presents his own assessment of the status of Jewish-Christians as if it were a minority view whereas Luke does not.

INDEX OF PASSAGES CITED

INDEX OF MODERN AUTHORS

When an author's name occurs more than once in the notes (pp. 118–29) I have indicated the number of occurrences in parenthesis.